Observing News and Media in a Complex Society

Sociocybernetics and Complexity

Volumes published in this Brill Research Perspectives title are listed at *brill.com/rpscs*

Observing News and Media in a Complex Society

A Sociocybernetic Perspective

By

Toru Takahashi

BRILL

LEIDEN | BOSTON

Library Congress Control Number: 2023950296

Typeface for the Latin, Greek, and Cyrillic scripts: "Brill". See and download: brill.com/brill-typeface.

ISSN 2772-2783
ISBN 978-90-04-69043-1 (paperback)
ISBN 978-90-04-69049-3 (e-book)
DOI 10.1163/9789004690493

Printed by Printforce, the Netherlands

Contents

Acknowledgements

The project of this book started in 2019 when I stayed in Bielefeld for my research on journalism studies. Chaime Marcuello-Servós, the editor of *Brill Research Perspectives in Sociocybernetics and Complexity*, kindly suggested writing this book and gave me encouraging feedback on my early manuscript. During my work on this project, I could have opportunities to discuss some parts of this book in Zaragoza, Urbino, Tokyo, and online. This book has profoundly benefited from critical and constructive comments from three reviewers working in the field of sociocybernetics. Fortunately, before finalizing the manuscript, I could discuss the problem of information overload, which is one of the key topics of this book, in sociocybernetic sessions held in Melbourne and online. I appreciate all the support and encouragement from my friends and colleagues.

Finally, I dedicate my humble work to my partner, Yuko. We have been living together for over twenty years. Talking with her sometimes strikes me with a wake-up hammer from the slumber of my habitual thinking.

Observing News and Media in a Complex Society

A Sociocybernetic Perspective

Toru Takahashi
Department of Political Science, Faculty of Law, Chuo University,
Tokyo, Japan
ttakahashi0@gmail.com

Abstract

This book discusses the conditions of news reporting in contemporary information-flooded society. As a sociological study, this book regards agenda-setting through news reporting as contributing to societal meaning construction. It is interested in its relations with other societal processes, such as politics and conflict. The author mainly draws upon strands of systems theoretical studies of the mass media, journalism, politics, terrorism, and armed conflict. In order to take a critical distance from such powerful societal forces and shed light on a practical, life-oriented dimension in civil society, this book discusses citizens' improvised efforts for problem-solving in their communities under the concept of governing. Finally, this book intends to expand our understanding of media's potential for supporting such bottom-up processes in society.

Keywords

news – media – journalism – problem-solving – communication – meaning – systems theory

•••

> I hear the same phrases in Odessa, Manila, Mexico City, New Jersey: 'There is so much information, misinformation, so much of everything that I don't know what's true any more.' Often I hear the phrase 'I feel the world is moving beneath my feet.' I catch myself thinking, 'I feel that everything that I thought solid is now unsteady, liquid.'
>
> PETER POMERANTSEV, *This Is Not Propaganda* (2019, p. xiii)

© TORU TAKAHASHI, 2024 | DOI:10.1163/9789004690493_002

•••

The critical spirit makes distinctions, and to distinguish is a sign of modernism.

UMBERTO ECO, *Ur-Fascism* (1995, June 22)

:·

Introduction

In 1937, a non-profit organization, the *Institute for Propaganda Analysis*, was established in New York. It laid out seven propaganda techniques to help citizens detect propagandistic materials (Manning, 2004, p. 140; Sproule, 1997, p. 135).[1] In the context of communication research, 1937 is remembered as the year of establishing the Office of Radio Research led by Paul F. Lazarsfeld, one of the founding fathers of communication research in the United States. Until television became common in living rooms in the 1950s, radio was the focus of early communication research. On October 31, 1938, the *New York Times* reported a panic incident caused by a radio drama based on H.G. Wells's novel *The War of the Worlds*. This incident later became the subject of Hadley Cantril's book *The Invasion from Mars* in 1940. The mass panic incident in Georgia stirred by fake television news of a Russian invasion in 2010 showed that the mass media could trigger such a nationwide storm in the twenty-first century. An early scholarly group, the *Communication Seminar*, which was organized in 1939 and produced the famous formulation of mass communication, "*who* says *what* in which *channel* to *whom* with what *effect*," had tension over its relation to wartime propaganda (Pooley, 2008, pp. 51–54).

The post-war era saw the rapid spread of television and politicians' adaptation to the new communication environment. Politicians found their opportunities for messaging strategy in short audiovisual clips called "sound bites" in television news on politics.[2] A catchy phrase such as "Income Doubling Plan" became a popular on-air slogan in news programs during the post-war economic growth in Japan (Feldman, 2004). In 1960, the first televised U.S.

---

1   The list of propagandistic techniques includes "name-calling," "glittering generalities," "transfer," "testimonial," "plain folks," "card stacking," and "bandwagon." See also Institute for Propaganda Analysis (1938:51).
2   See Bas and Grabe (2015) for the definition and brief history of the term.

presidential debate between John F. Kennedy and Richard Nixon gave the impression that the election became a media event on television. Several years after the debate, the war in Vietnam was televised and brought into the living rooms (Arlen, 1982). The connection between the result of the war and television's effect on public opinion was widely believed in the United States and prompted the British government to restrict press access to the Falkland Islands campaign in 1982 (Mandelbaum, 1982; Harris, 1983). Meanwhile, researchers have been studying the effect of television on public opinion. In the mid-1980s, Daniel C. Hallin succinctly described the change in the research community's perception of the media effect. "Very few media researchers today accept the 'minimal effect' view that dominated academic media research in the 1950s and early 1960s. A growing number of studies confirm the commonsense idea that television – and other media – can indeed … shape political perceptions very powerfully" (Hallin, 1986, p. 108).

In the early 1990s, the Internet was the new frontier of networking and creativity for scientific researchers and curious early comers. After those old happy days, it became a place of daily conversations and a new platform for e-commerce. As the user community grew, online service providers such as AOL faced the problem of the growing cost of moderation.[3] In the 2000s, using social media and writing blog posts became essential for many people's daily lives, especially the native digital generation familiar with digital devices from early childhood. This expansion of media communication in online public space has increased the amount, speed, and variety of communication. Today, we also observe that the Internet has become a fierce battlefield of political interests and ideologies. Big social media platforms like *Facebook* and *Twitter/X* are under pressure to be more responsible for the impact of political posts.

Social scientists have been interested in the social and political consequences of the tidal wave of information. Looking back at the historical experience in Europe, Niklas Luhmann discussed the impact of the printing press on the sociocultural evolution of ideas. The printing press enhanced storage capacity and made traditional mnemonics obsolete. Knowledge, thoughts, and beliefs printed in books can be compared to others (Luhmann, 2012, p. 328). In the early twentieth century, Charles H. Cooley (1962, p. 93) wrote that the modern conditions of communication enlarged "the competition of ideas," and any ideas could not elude comparison with others. Max Weber (2004, p. 243) discussed the "meaninglessness" (Sinnlosigkeit) in modern society, where striving for self-perfection (or self-realization) through creating and learning cultural contents had become improbable to be accomplished in our

---

3 For the case of the AOL volunteer moderators and their labor problem, see Postigo (2009).

finite life.[4] Felix Geyer and colleagues discussed the problem of "alienation" in the complex information-driven society, which requires individual autonomy and identity to have more flexible structures (Geyer, 1980; Geyer, 1996; Geyer & Schweitzer, 1976, 1981; Geyer & Heinz, 1992). Geyer observed that the modern (and "postmodern") society raised the problem of meaninglessness among individuals. He writes, "With the accelerating throughput of information, ... meaninglessness is not a matter anymore of whether one can assign meaning to incoming information, but of whether one can develop adequate new scanning mechanism to gather the goal-relevant information one needs, as well as more efficient selection procedures to prevent being overburdened by the information one does not need" (Geyer, 1996, p. xxxii).

Figure 1 shows a century trend of the estimated amount of information consumption in Japan. It significantly grew in periods after the late 1950s and 1980s. As we will see later (3.1), (at first black-and-white, then color) television sets spread in the former period. In the late 1970s, Jean Baudrillard observed the problematic relation between information and meaning. "We live in a world where there is more and more information, and less and less meaning" (Baudrillard, 1994, p. 79). He saw the destruction of the order of meaning in the movement of the avant-garde in art, such as dada, and the literature of the absurd,[5] and discussed the saturation of "simulacra," or images which have no relation to any reality. Observing American society after the proliferation of television sets reached a plateau, Doris A. Graber wrote, "We live in an age of information glut" (Graber, 1984, p. 1). The latter period of the consumption hike (the late 1980s) was mainly a result of the development of digital data transmission services for businesses and consumers. Today's information processing technology has furthermore enhanced the comparability of ideas. Anthony Giddens would describe this situation as a digitalized version of "high modernity" or "post-traditional society" (Giddens, 1991; Beck et al., 1994). Zygmunt Bauman's (2000) "liquid society" and Lars Qvortrup's (2003) "hypercomplex society" are other names for the circumstances of digital modernity.

---

4   Agreed with Alois Hahn (1987), Luhmann (1987, p. 322) stated that meaninglessness (Sinnlosigkeit) is experienced when a system fails in self-description. We may say that the problem is a correlative of individualization that urges individuals to find narratives of their own lives. Today, we also see problems of group identities invoked by political discourse, such as nationalism, and struggles of antiracism, feminism, and sexual minorities.

5   However, for the author of *The Myth of Sisyphus*, the absurd meant that we are facing the unmanageable complexity of the world that cannot be sorted out by reason. The complexity is not a sign of a disintegrated world but the initial condition of our life. "It was previously a question of finding out whether or not life had to have a meaning to be lived. It now becomes clear on the contrary that it will be lived all the better if it has no-meaning" (Camus, 1975, p. 53).

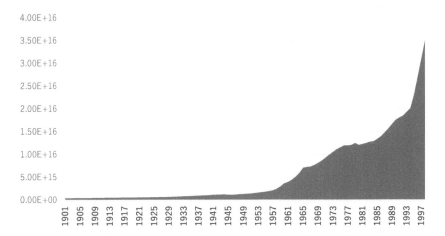

FIGURE 1   Estimated amount of information consumption in Japan in the 20th century
SOURCE: THE 2000 WHITE PAPER "COMMUNICATIONS IN JAPAN"
(MINISTRY OF POSTS AND TELECOMMUNICATIONS)

Facing the tidal wave of scattered, sometimes deceiving information, people can never feel that they live in the cosmos of meanings, or under the "sacred canopy" (Berger, 1967) of tradition. We do not stand on the steady ground of an unshakable body of meanings. So, we must keep communicating and constantly rebuilding meanings in and of our lives.[6] A brief and general definition of communication from a cybernetic point of view is that it is interaction (conversation) by signals between at least two observing systems (participants) who observe and construct understandings of each other (Scott, 2021, p. 39). In this book, I will focus on *inter-human communication* as a key process of the social construction of meaning.[7] By "meaning," I mean ideas presented and interpreted in communication. Whereas "information" brings something new, something different, or something irritating to a system and the novelty starts to wear off as it is experienced, meaning does not conflict with reuse and familiarity (Bateson, 2000; Luhmann, 1995). In this respect, meaning appears as an object referred to and thematized in communication. Meaning is often

---

6 Here we may discuss the "rationalization of the lifeworld" (Habermas, 1987, p. 288). However, this book is more interested in describing an empirical condition of today's lifeworld than searching for an ideal procedure to reach a socially accepted meaning.

7 Scholars interested in a description diversified in terms of agencies may try another concept such as "network," which is a string of actions where (both human and non-human) actors are doing something (Latour, 2005, p. 128). I do not exclude a description of non-human actors like machines and AIs, but I will follow the directive of sociocybernetics: observe the observer.

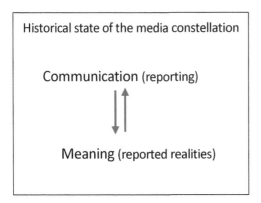

FIGURE 2
Communication and the media
constellation

united to our personal or collective beliefs and feelings. Meaning is also con-
ceived as a description of the world, society, group, and personality. Meaning is
a joint product of biological, psychological, and social processes. "Meaning is
biological, cultural, individually experienced, and situated" (Brier, 2008, p. 101).
Meaning is anchored in our life, and our life is anchored in the symbolic order
of society through meaning. However, meaning is ultimately a social product.
Communication is the only place where meaning is created, reconstructed,
and sometimes broken down as a result of human interaction.[8]

As sketched above, media and society (including politics and conflict) are
intertwined with each other. We cannot ignore the impact of *media and information technology*, which has enormously enhanced our communication in
terms of space, speed, and quantity. This has brought about various consequences in the public sphere of communication because people do what they
can technologically do in communication (Rempel, 2001, p. 91). Hence, I consider the historical state of the constellation, or a matrix of accessible media of
the times, as societal and technological conditions of the meaning construction and circulation of realities reported by journalists (Figure 2).

In Part 1, I will look into a theoretical dialogue on communication between
Heinz von Foerster and Niklas Luhmann (von Foerster, 2003; Luhmann, 1991,
1993). The dialogue went through critical points of communication theory
from the perspectives of second-order cybernetics and the sociological theory
of social systems. In a general context, "sociocybernetics" is defined as the sociological application of systems science and cybernetics (Hornung, 2019, p. 511).

---

8   Here I will not discuss indescribable experience and insight such as "the sense of the world"
    (*Tractatus*, 6.41) in Wittgenstein's sense, which lies outside the scientifically described world
    (Wittgenstein, 2014, p. 86). However, this does not exclude that one tries to put the incom-
    municable in one's own words.

In the recent decade, sociocybernetics has been addressing social phenomena and problems relevant to this book, such as the impact of the changing media environment and problematic information (e.g., Boccia Artieri & Gemini, 2019; Taekke, 2019, 2022; Giglietto et al., 2019), politics and conflict (e.g., Takahashi, 2015a; Mitchell, 2016; Mancilla, 2020; Paeteau, 2019), knowledge and culture (e.g., González et al., 2016; Leydesdorff, 2021; Maass, 2018; Sidorova et al., 2020). Sociocybernetics has also proposed that interdependence between different social spheres should be examined in order to tackle societal challenges today (Marcuello-Servós, 2018). This book intends to discuss media and journalism, considering the implications of politics, conflict, and societal efforts for problem-solving. Communication and social construction of meaning give a common framework for the entire project.

Von Foerster showed his fundamental model of communication between two autonomous units ("non-trivial machines") and discussed the importance of recursiveness for communication and its "Eigen value" formation. Luhmann stressed that communication is another type of autopoietic system that produces itself through its own operation. This book sets out a sociocybernetic perspective that sees communication as a cybernetic process that forms its eigenvalues and steers itself by its recursive operation. After taking the first step into the problem of communication, I will discuss the social construction of meaning in the process of societal efforts for problem-solving under the concepts of *steering* and *governance*. Steering and governability have been traditional topics in sociocybernetics (e.g., Geyer & van der Zouwen, 1986; Gibson, 2007). Concepts such as *autopoiesis* of social systems were applied to these subjects (in't Veld et al., 1991). In parallel with the trend in sociocybernetics, governance studies discussed the limit of steering by the state and its government (Rosenau & Czempiel, 1992; Rhodes, 1997; Pierre & Peters, 2000).[9] This insight suggests the importance of bottom-up processes of problem-solving and prompts scholars to think about governance as societal networking. "Public management is mainly the governance of complex networks of many different participants, such as governmental organisations, political and social groups, institutions, private and business organisations" (Kickert, 1993, p. 191).[10]

---

9   Interestingly, John H. Little (2001) discussed the possibility of steering government by the public.

10 R.A.W. Rhodes discussed the most network-centered model of governance. "'Governance' means there is no one centre but multiple centres; there is no sovereign authority because networks have significant autonomy. The distinction between the public, private and voluntary section becomes meaningless" (Rhodes, 1997, p. 109). The vision of a "centreless society" (Rhodes, 1997, p. 3) refers to Luhmann's description of the modern functionally differentiated society, which does not regard any societal subsystem as a center of

The concept of governance now covers activities that involve governmental and non-governmental actors. "Governing can be considered as the totality of interactions, in which public as well as private actors participate, aimed at solving societal problems or creating societal opportunities" (Kooiman, 2003, p. 4). Undoubtedly, such interactions are interesting for sociologists as well.

Governance needs a framework that underpins and regulates participants' cooperation. However, it does not need to be authorized by legal and political power, especially in cases such as international cooperation and voluntary activities in neighborhoods. Actors can communicate with each other and establish their shared goals and action programs. The theory of autopoietic social systems may regard governance as a self-organizational process of communication for problem-solving in society. The theory tends to underline the autonomy of communicative processes and therefore finds only self-governing or -steering of systems (Luhmann, 1997, p. 48). Then, if a social system steers itself, what does it steer in its communicative process? Eva Buchinger (2007) notes that the object of steering in social systems is not concrete actors but differences which systems use for processing meaning. Through communicative processes, social systems define social problems, establish shared goals, and approve new bills. Steering in communication takes a form of recursive intervention based upon second-order observation. Here I will set aside personal issues, such as troubles in intimate and family relationships, and focus on public concerns that need our efforts. The process of such collective efforts will be discussed under the concept of *governing* (1.4). I believe that problem-solving is a key part of the social construction of meaning because it cannot be successful without discussing and building common goals and values in society. This book will think about governing in the circumstances of a complex society equipped with digital media technology. In the second half of Part 1, I will introduce Jan Kooiman's governance theory, which provides a useful taxonomy to describe the elemental aspects of governance (Kooiman, 2003).

---

society, unlike statist and the so-called base and superstructure models. The effectiveness of state- and society-centered models should be examined in practical contexts. For the types of governance model, see also Pierre (2000, p. 3).

Instead of a network-based approach, Michael Rempel (2001) developed the concept of "interpenetration" to describe the joint participation of multiple subsystems in social deliberations.

Walter Lippmann critically mentioned that an ideal model of journalism supposes that journalists should look at the whole society and report all important news that good citizens should keep in their minds (Lippmann, 2018). For Lippmann, considering the complexity of society, it is an impossible task for journalists and a delusion about citizens' competence. "We misunderstand the limited nature of news, the illimitable complexity of society, we overestimate our own endurance, public spirit, and all-around competence. … If the newspapers, then, are to be charged with the duty of translating the whole public life of mankind, so that every adult can arrive at an opinion on every moot topic, they fail, … It is not possible to assume that a world, carried on by division of labor and distribution of authority, can be governed by universal opinion in the whole population" (Lippmann, 2018, p. 155). He argued that we could not define journalism's role without considering the complexity of the differentiated society.

The vision of the complex society posed by Lippmann can be redescribed from the systems theoretical perspective. Elisabeth Noelle-Neumann mentioned that Niklas Luhmann treated the same subject, the complexity of modern society, in the framework of his sociological theory (Noelle-Neumann, 1984, p. 146). Luhmann found the characteristics of modern society in its structural differentiation: functional differentiation. This multipolar structure has brought about the incongruity of perspectives between societal subsystems. In this book, the adjective "societal" will be used when I refer to processes and activities relevant or potentially relevant to a whole society. Besides the possible incongruity among views of individuals and organizations, functional differentiation is the primary background of the complexity in modern society.

In Part 2, I will look into the movement of systems theoretical studies of journalism, which tried to redefine journalism's societal role and autonomy in the functionally differentiated society. The systems theorists discussed that the multipolar structure of modern society created the need for something that bridges gaps between societal subsystems. One of the most important tasks of social systems theory is to describe how a system forms its boundary against its environment. Indeed, this has been the most challenging task for systems theorists in this field. Journalism is one of the communicative activities which construct publicly shared meanings. Importantly, knowledge of agendas and events reported by journalists creates preconditions for problem-solving.

The meaning construction through news coverage and its reception by the public does not take place in a disconnected place from other social forces such as politics. Looking back to Britain in the seventeenth century, royalist and parliamentarian newsbooks waged a battle for public opinion (Brownlees,

2006, pp. 17–20). In the twentieth century, the battlefield moved from political pamphlets to the mass media. Since then, news media and politics have been closely interacting with each other. Part 3 will focus on the process of political communication and its relation to the mass media, especially journalism. Along with describing the interrelation between politics and the mass media, I will look into the findings of *populism* studies, which will help us figure out politicians' messaging strategies on media platforms. As political communication is often conducted in the form of conflict, I will also discuss the communicative process of conflict. Luhmann (1995) pointed out a "parasitic" nature of conflict, which lives on the resources of its host society but can be destructive to it. In the most severe forms, such as *terrorism* and *armed conflict*, conflict becomes profoundly devastating, especially when it involves the entire population and damages multiple dimensions of society. Politicians and conflicting parties are motivated to disseminate messages through the media in order to share their own views. On the other hand, journalistic autonomy has a performative involvement with politics and conflict (Cottle, 2006). This media-politics/conflict interaction inevitably affects the societal construction of realities and, consequently, governing efforts. Systems theoretical studies of *terrorism* and *armed conflict* have tried to describe the autonomy of their communicative processes and destructive effects on society. I will discuss these forms of conflict and their relations to society in the second half of Part 3. Figure 3 shows the structure of the study in this book.

The 2000s was an epoch toward the age of social media and smartphones. Major social media platforms were launched in the mid-2000s (*Facebook* in 2004, *YouTube* in 2005, and *Twitter* in 2006). *iPhone* and the first device equipped with the *Android* OS released in 2007 and 2008. According to a survey conducted by the *Pew Research Center*, 86% of American people (often or

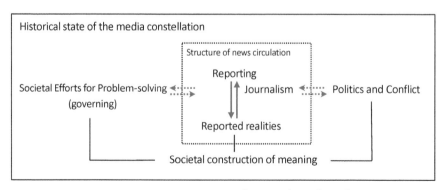

FIGURE 3   Reporting as meaning construction under societal interdependence

sometimes) use a smartphone, computer, or tablet to get news. In contrast, traditional mass media have less chance to be used for the purpose (television 68%, radio 50%, print publication 32%) (Shearer, 2021). The current circumstances of the communication environment have raised the question of whether we are witnessing a structural change in news circulation and agenda-setting processes. Based on the findings of intermedia agenda-setting studies, I will discuss the current structure of news circulation in the age of social media. This is the main topic of the first half of Part 4.

As the number of participants in online communication grew and the incongruity of perspectives became increasingly visible, news reporting became more controversial. Every news article is a product of a series of "selections" in the editing process. Lippmann wrote, "Every newspaper when it reaches the reader is the result of a whole series of selections as to what items shall be printed, in what position they shall be printed, how much space each shall occupy, what emphasis each shall have" (Lippmann, 2018, p. 152). Readers may have different views on each decision of the selection procedure. Their views become public as soon as they are expressed on the Internet. Journalists' selections can always be compared with other possibilities. This contemporary condition of news reception prompts us to update our understanding and description of what news is. The second half of Part 4 will discuss Dirk Baecker's (2005) concept of news and try to redescribe the condition of news reporting.

Every governing is a precautionary or reactive effort to deal with a collective problem. Governing is organized through communication and networking between multiple actors involved in a problem. Journalism contributes to tackling problems by making the public aware of social issues and possibly persuading the people and the government to take action on them. In many cases, the government is the most powerful actor in terms of budget, human resources, and legitimacy in public governance. However, the hegemony of journalism and the government in information dissemination and problem-solving has become debatable. The Internet has become a powerful civic media platform. The government is not the only actor who makes a difference in problem-solving. Politicians who lead policy-making are also busy sending political messages to voters through their words circulating through the media. This nature of politics can be an obstacle to taking proper measures. People can improve their understanding of social problems through online communication. However, learning about an issue and taking action are different stages for problem-solving. Part 5 will focus on the dimension of collective efforts to solve social problems and the supportive role of the media. Media technology can be used not only for disseminating information but also for more practical purposes such as fundraising and recruiting staff. This means that media can play a bridging role in sharing information and building cooperation. So, we need a concept of media that understands the media's societal roles in broader contexts (Takahashi, 2015b, 2019). The mass media and so-called social media have been utilized for consuming spectacles and political control. However, that is not everything media can offer to society. The sociocybernetic perspective presented in this book instead sees the media's potential for problem-solving on the ground.

Summing up, this book discusses the conditions of news coverage in constructing meaning, considering the historical changes of the societal media constellation. As a sociological study, this book regards agenda-setting through news reporting as contributing to societal meaning construction and is interested in its relations with other societal domains. This book also considers politics and conflict as they constitute autonomous processes of communication and the influential societal environment of news coverage and its reception. For this study, the author mainly draws upon strands of systems theoretical studies of the mass media, journalism, politics, terrorism, and armed conflict. In order to take a critical distance from such powerful societal forces and shed light on a practical, life-oriented dimension in civil society, this book discusses citizens' improvised efforts for problem-solving in their communities under the concept of governing. Finally, this book intends to expand our understanding of the potential of media for supporting such bottom-up processes in society.

Part 1: Cybernetics and Communication

1.1 *Communication and Recursivity*

Human interaction has been discussed as the basal process of human society in strands of sociocybernetic theories. Humberto R. Maturana found the function of linguistic interaction in giving orientation to interacting organisms within their cognitive domains. He observed that consensus arises through the process of cooperative inter-orientation and subsequent orienting interactions take place within their consensual domains. He argued that the "transmission" model of communication is a kind of illusion because it entirely depends on the establishment of consensus among interacting organisms (Maturana & Varela, 1980, pp. 30–35). Maturana stressed the importance of being an observer as an outsider of established social orders. "Conduct as observer by a human being implies that he stands operationally as if outside the various social systems that he otherwise integrates, and that he may undergo in this manner interactions that do not confirm them. An observer always is potentially antisocial" (Maturana & Varela, 1980, p. xxviii). Even though society is organized by participation of human individuals, it can be both humane and inhumane. Maturana sees that society has its own logic toward stabilization. He writes, "the relations that undergo historical stabilization are those that have to do with the stability of the society as a unity in a given medium, and not with the well-being of its component human beings that may operate as observers" (Maturana & Varela, 1980, p. xxviii). The tense relations between established stabilities and critical observers come to the surface in every corner of society. This is a permanent factor of social dynamics.

In his study of alienation in modern society, Felix Geyer (1976, 1980) formulated his model of an information processing system, which has a boundary between itself and its environment. An outside observer can see that the system is processing incoming stimuli (inputs) from its environment but cannot see what exactly happens inside the system ("black box"). The observer can also see that the system behaves in its environment (outputs). Geyer thinks that this model is applicable to both individuals and groups. However, for his purpose of alienation study, he focused on human individuals and their relations with social environments. Based on the framework, Geyer discussed the problem of alienation and meaninglessness as information processing problems on the level of individuals. "Meaning is primarily assigned to incoming potential information by coding it, i.e. by giving it a specific place in the network of information stored already. ... Meaninglessness is therefore the result of the (personality) system's subjectively felt inability to assign meaning to new inputs" (Geyer, 1976, p. 198). Individuals feel alienated when they cannot exercise their initiative in processing information. This is very likely to happen under an oppressive regime such as a totalitarian society, as Maturana (Maturana & Varela, 1980, p. xxviii) mentioned. In the early 1990s, Geyer and Walter R. Heinz (1992, p. xxxii) pointed out that the problem of information overload and alienation may increase relevance in the complex information-driven society.

Gordon Pask expanded the class of entities, which, having their own perspectives, participate in conversation. Conversation takes place between participants A and B in a language. Here "participants" are specified as "coherent and stable conceptual systems" (Pask, 1978, p. 17). So, as far as coherent and stable perspectives are distinctly observed, we can deal with a variety of conversing entities such as cultures, schools of thought, and social institutions. He writes, "we must seriously countenance the integrity and individuality of these perspective-having entities ... cultures A and B may 'converse', or people may converse with cultures" (Pask, 1978, pp. 17–18). Through joining in conversation, those entities begin a learning process to come to know each other.[11] This may eventually result in some stability in the relationship of conversing entities. However, if we see life as an enduring learning process, stability should always be improvised practically in a given context. Building learning processes in our communities is an important angle to reconsider journalism and media as more socially oriented activities and technology.

In February 1993, Heinz von Foerster gave a lecture on communication in a colloquium that celebrated Niklas Luhmann's sixty-fifth birthday. Von Foerster discussed the importance of recursivity for communication and showed his basic model of communication (von Foerster, 2003). Von Foerster started his talk by introducing two types of machines that sociocyberneticians are already familiar with, "trivial machines" and "non-trivial machines." A "trivial machine" always gives its output in the same way (like a simple calculator, which adds two every time it gets input from its operator). So, one can precisely predict how it works. However, it is impossible to predict how a non-trivial machine behaves because its inner states are constantly changing. Von Foerster (2003, pp. 314–315) gave an interesting tweak to the model of a non-trivial machine. He added a recursive circuit through which the machine's output runs into itself (Figure 4). We may be able to use this model to describe human behavior. We are constantly hearing and reading what we talk about and write. We calibrate our behavior through this self-monitoring. The most important implication of the recursive model is that, according to von Foerster, a stable value emerges as a result of the machine's recursive operation. He said, "through this recursive closure and only through this recursive closure do stabilities arise that could never be discovered through input/output analysis" (von Foerster, 2003, p. 316). He argues that recursivity is the only way to reach a stable pattern for a complex machine. However, this single-unit model still represents a monologue. We need another step to build a communicative model.

Von Foerster (2003, pp. 317–318) combined two recursive machines and called this new system "composition" (Figure 5). In composition, each machine receives input from itself and the other combined machine. These two machines can, to some extent, steer each other through this exchange.

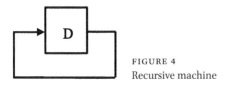

FIGURE 4
Recursive machine

---

11   For the implication of learning in Pask's theory, see Scott (2001).

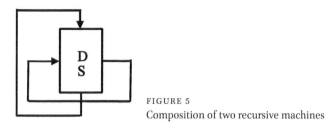

FIGURE 5
Composition of two recursive machines

A sociologically important question on this "composition" model is whether recursivity would produce stable values, which he calls "Eigen behaviors," also in this more complex system. Von Foerster gave a positive answer to this question. He formulated his thought in the theorem: "In every operationally closed system there arise Eigen behaviors" (von Foerster, 2003, p. 321).

In conclusion, von Foerster defined communication as a stable dynamic. He said, "Communication is the Eigen behavior of a recursively operating system that is doubly closed onto itself" (von Foerster, 2003, p. 322). In his lecture, he gave us another insight into communication. He thought we could not find out what generated an eigenbehavior in communication. What we can see is that communication runs recursively and produces stable patterns (von Foerster, 2003, p. 317). For von Foerster, this impossibility of identifying an exact cause of an eigenbehavior has an ethical implication. We cannot know a decisive factor that brought about an eigenbehavior in communication. All we can say is that people who take part in the communicative process are responsible for its results. This *responsibility* is the condition of our freedom and autonomy. If we don't take responsibility, von Foerster says, we will let someone decide and obey the decision (von Foerster, 2003, pp. 286, 322).

1.2   *Communication as a Social System*
Luhmann responded to von Foerster from his sociological perspective. The dialogue between the two theorists has a prehistory. In 1991, two years before the colloquium, Luhmann wrote a contribution to the book, which celebrated von Foerster's eightieth birthday (Luhmann, 1991). He discussed that we can treat a social system as an observer if we understand that communicative processes also conduct observation. Drawing on George Spencer-Brown's (2021) logic, Luhmann formulated observation as handling distinctions (Luhmann, 1995, p. 36) and argued that distinctions can be made by communicative processes. He also mentioned that von Foerster would not welcome this concept of communication as a social system. Sociology has the tradition of studying society as "reality sui generis" (Durkheim, 2001, p. 17). Charles H. Cooley (1962, p. 64) depicted that through participating in communication the mind creates

social structures, which have unignorable effects on it: "if we take a larger view and consider the life of a social group, we see that communication, including its organization into literature, art, and institutions, is truly the outside or visible structure of thought ... the symbols, the traditions, the institutions are projected from the mind, ... but in the very instant of their projection, ... they react upon it, and in a sense control it, stimulating, developing, and fixing certain thoughts." Social structures emerge from bottom-up processes, and once established, they exercise hierarchical control on subsequent social processes (Geyer, 1996, p. xxii). In the context of the sociological tradition, understanding communication as an autonomous system can be seen as another version of exploration of the social. However, in von Foerster's view, the sociological theory is problematic because it attributes communicative actions not only to persons but also to the system of communication.

Despite the difference, on the basal level of communication, Luhmann finds a "dialogical constitution," which reminds us of von Foerster's "composition" model. He writes, "self-reference on the level of basal processes is possible only if at least two processing units that operate with information are present and if they can relate to each other and thereby to themselves" (Luhmann, 1995, p. 138). Searching for prerequisites of social systems, Talcott Parsons (2012) worked on this basal condition of social interaction. He pointed out that recursive, or "double" contingency on "cues" exchanged in social interaction is the essential element that gives a chance to form a stable pattern in communication. Ego and alter expect each other's actions in their interaction. If both intend to build a good or at least tolerable relationship instead of breaking with each other, one's actions should be experienced as "sanctions," which prompt or inhibit particular reactions of the other, and vice versa. When one receives a positive response from the other, one may think that the interaction is going smoothly, at least for the moment. However, the intransparency of future developments can never be removed from the relationship. Referring to von Foerster's principle of "order from noise" (von Foerster, 2003, p. 13), Luhmann discussed that this basal condition gives a chance to invent a stable pattern of communication. In the face of uncertainty in communication, ego and alter, seeking clues to decide their own actions, observe each other carefully (Luhmann, 1995, pp. 104–105). We may also involve ourselves in "immediate" interaction by expressing our feelings or thoughts without planning or internal simulation of the other (Geyer, 1980, pp. 128–129). This will give us some experience that can be applied later to anticipate alter's response. Erving Goffman (1959, p. 1) writes, "observers can glean clues from his conduct and appearance which allow them to apply their previous experience with individuals roughly similar to the one before them." Reactively or spontaneously, we may continue to communicate and find some transparency, but the other will remain a source of unexpectedness.[12] Here, a problem, the uncertainty in this case, serves as a catalyst for persevering efforts to proceed with communicative interaction.

In order to articulate the prerequisites of communication and social order, Parsons discussed two aspects. The first is a stable "symbolic system of meanings," which is a prerequisite for understandability in communication. He thought that communication between multiple actors would not last long unless the stable symbolic system is generalized or abstracted from particular situations. He writes: "The most important single implication of this generalization is perhaps the possibility of communication, because the situations of two actors are *never* identical and without the capacity to abstract meaning from the most particular situations communication would be impossible" (Parsons, 2012, p. 6, emphasis in the original). Once a stable symbolic system established, which Parsons called "cultural tradition," ego and alter can expect that their messages will be understood as intended though misunderstanding is still probable. The second aspect is related to the function of the norm, or value standards, on which actors evaluate their selection from alternative orientations. "These standards are ... a particularly crucial part of the cultural tradition of the social system" (Parsons, 2012, pp. 25–26). The cultural tradition – in another phrase, a "system of culturally structured and shared symbols" (Parsons, 2012, p. 3) – is the prerequisite of communication and its order.

Luhmann embarked on building his theory of communication systems, which covers a systems theoretical concept of communication and a multi-layered concept of media. We may say that he advanced a "communicative turn" in the sociological theory of social systems.[13] He formulated three constitutive elements of communication (*information as a communicated message, act of presenting a message such as utterance,* and *understanding by a partner*) and defined communication as a three-part selection process (Luhmann, 1995, pp. 139–145). One can decide what to communicate and how to present a message to a partner. The message has to be received and understood as a communicated message by the partner to become a part of the communicative

---

12   Hofmannsthal's homecomer, who felt like he had lost his footing in modernity, also built a practical attitude to deal with communication (Hofmannsthal, 1991). For Hofmannsthal's and sociological, especially Simmel's description of modernity, see Robertson (2007).

13   "Communicative turn" is often mentioned in the contexts of theoretical development of both Luhmann and Habermas in the 1980s (Harste, 2021).

process. Non-communicative phenomena, such as thinking aloud and notes in book margins, are recognized as those in the environment of the communicative process. Luhmann thought that a communication system distinguishes itself from its environment by distinguishing between the communicative and the non-communicative.

The three elements of communication imply problems of improbabilities in communication. First, due to various factors like distance, environmental noise, and malfunction of communication tools, it is not sure that messages will reach intended receivers correctly (*reachability*). This was the main concern of Shannon and Weaver's classical model of communication (Shannon & Weaver, 1963).[14] Second, receivers may interpret the message in unexpected ways or even find difficulty in understanding (*understandability*). Third, it depends on receivers whether the given information will be accepted as premises for their subsequent communication (*acceptability*).

Luhmann (1995, pp. 147–150, 157–163) distinguished three different types of "media" which deal with these improbabilities (reachability, understandability, and acceptability). *Language* serves to understand messages in communication, but we cannot exclude the possibility of misunderstanding. *Media of dissemination*, such as the printing press and broadcasting media, bridge spatial and temporal distance between communicating partners. Today, many kinds of media are digitalized and, more importantly, at hand for citizens. This has enhanced individuals' capability to disseminate messages in public communication. *Symbolically generalized communication media* motivate an addressee to accept what the addressee understands as a premise of subsequent behavior. But the addressee is not necessarily fully motivated by this type of media. People may sometimes hide different thoughts and pretend to accept an imparted message. However, even in that case, acceptability can still be observed and anticipated at the communicative level. This reveals that the mental process and communication run separately.

As seen above, the function of generalized symbols in communication was initially discussed by Talcott Parsons. Laying stress on acceptance, Luhmann (2012, p. 191) borrowed the formula *"symbolically generalized"* from Parsons in his theory of communication media. "In the context of the 'symbolically generalized communication media' concept, I therefore (like Parsons) mean

---

14   More precisely, this is the technical problem at "Level A" of communication problems. Warren Weaver also formulated the semantic ("Level B") and the effectiveness ("Level C") problems of communication (Shannon & Weaver, 1963, p. 4). We can see parallels between Weaver's three levels and Luhmann's three improbabilities. Drawing on Weaver's distinction, Loet Leydesdorff and his colleagues developed the operationalized approach to information processing and meaning construction (e.g., Leydesdorff et al., (2017)).

by 'symbolic' that these media bridge a difference and supply communication with opportunities for acceptance" (Luhmann, 2012, p. 192). He mentions several examples of this type of communication media, such as legitimate *power*, *truth*, and *money*. These media work in different and specific situations. When the government sends a message that one should submit a document by a fixed deadline, it is highly likely that one accepts it and submits the document, though it is still possible to ignore the message. There are uncountable studies, but we do not accept all of them as "scientific" and their findings as "truth." Findings must be obtained through proper scientific research methods and procedures to be taken as verified. Luhmann called the criteria which control the allocation of positive and negative values of specific *binary codes* – in science, "true" and "not true" – *"programs"* (Luhmann, 2012, pp. 215–218; Luhmann 1990a, p. 197). By the binary code and programs, science distinguishes itself and its communication environment, namely scientific communication and other categories of communication. These two apparatuses are pivotal for describing the autonomy of societal subsystems of modern society (for the application in journalism studies, see 2.3).

The *"basic values,"* such as human rights, also provide communication with acceptability (Luhmann, 1995, p. 161, 2012, p. 247). One can expect that a discourse based on a fundamental value like equality will be accepted and supported in communication. Like symbolically generalized communication media, values work as frames of reference to sort out acceptable messages. It is not difficult to see whether a remark is supportive or not of a particular value. So, as we find plenty of examples on social media, there are a variety of moral communication and even disputes over the correctness of remarks in our daily conversation. Also, in more public and professional spheres of communication like politics, business, science, and sports, opinions and behaviors are constantly examined from ethical points of view. Journalism often undertakes moral observation, especially of the power elite and celebrities.

Communication, handling these three improbabilities, constantly processes meaning. Sociology has been interested in this process. Alfred Schutz discussed the construction of common-sense knowledge and shed light on our experience and interpretation of knowledge. "All interpretation of this world is based on a stock of previous experiences of it, our own or those handed down to us by parents or teachers" (Schutz, 1971, p. 7). There is a cycle of experience and interpretation in constructing common knowledge. As time goes by, meanings get detached from original contexts, or "symbolically generalized," and become available in various contexts. Borrowing the word "sedimentation" from Schutz and Edmund Husserl, Peter L. Berger and Thomas Luckmann described this process of meaning construction. "Intersubjective sedimentation can be called truly social only when it has been objectivated in a sign system of one kind or another, that is, when the possibility of reiterated objectification of the shared experiences arises" (Berger & Luckmann, 1980, p. 63).

The construction of meaning happens under the basal condition of communication discussed by von Foerster, Parsons, and Luhmann. Luhmann writes, "meaning arises and is reproduced in certain (consciousness and social) systems as 'eigenbehavior'" (Luhmann, 2012, p. 23). An eigenbehavior emerges as a result of a recursive process in communication. Communication runs and steers itself by referring to its past and future. It also uses the stock of meanings conveyed through media or handed down from past generations. The stock of meanings includes a body of ideas proven to be recognizable through reiterated use in communication. Luhmann calls a stabilized meaning, which has matured "in a process of reuse, concentration, abstraction" and provides communication with predictability, *semantics* (Luhmann, 2012, p. 190).[15] For sociocybernetics, semantics can be understood as reusable eigenvalues (eigenbehaviors) generated through the recursive process of communication. In this book, an *eigenbehavior* will mean a recognizable pattern of communication, and an *eigenvalue* will refer to a recognizable meaning created through the communicative process.

Today, various algorithms are working on the web. We know that we are enclosed in personalized recommendation systems of platform companies. The cage of comfortable information termed a "filter bubble" (Pariser, 2011) is formed through a positive feedback loop of personalization.[16] However, this does not change the fundamental conditions of our web communication. Elena Esposito (2017, p. 293) sees here virtual interaction with computed profiles of ourselves. "What the user is interacting with through digital technology is his own reflected and revised contingency. In a sense the user communicates with himself in an unrecognizable and surprising form." Indeed, interacting with a complex of our past selections is not authentic communication. But it is still interesting, as a fundamental question, whether the basic condition of communication, which von Foerster formulated in his model of non-trivial machines' composition and Luhmann discussed through his reconsideration

---

15   For the definition and function of "semantics" in social systems, see also Luhmann (1980).
16   Giovanni Boccia Artieri and Laura Gemini (2019) describe Facebook as an autonomous sphere of communication because of its algorithm and the individuals' significant role in generating the content (a characteristic of so-called Web 2.0). But the autonomy is distinguished from that of functional systems such as the mass media system in Luhmann's sense (see 2.2).

of Parsons' concept of double contingency, could apply to the human-machine interaction. However, as the program of the Turing Test shows, the observation of human-machine interaction is, at least thus far, initiated and conducted from the human side. This makes it difficult to think about the authenticity of a human-machine interaction that looks like communication. It should be a problem of a practical, ultimately ethical decision whether we regard a machine as a communicative partner.[17]

In his contribution to the birthday volume for von Foerster, Luhmann (1991, p. 71) raised an intriguing question about eigenvalues: Can (or must) we suppose formation of latent eigenvalues? Luhmann suggests that this question unfolds at first- and second-order observation levels. Latency at the first-order level hides an eigenvalue behind observations. We cannot or simply do not observe the latent eigenvalue which decides the observations and their objects. At this level, we cannot get behind the surface as a dreamer "cannot, unless close to waking, dream a statement referring to (i.e., framing) his dream" (Bateson, 2000, p. 185). How at all does society dream like individuals? And if it does, how can society awake from its dream? It is true that "we do not see what we do not see." Von Foerster (2003, p. 284) argued that this "second order deficiency" can be healed by finding new paradigms as Europe awoke from the Ptolemaic dream. Scholars in media studies conceptualized media frames as "latent" structures of meaning and discussed framing devices such as news values, strategy- and issue-oriented discourse (D'Angelo, 2017, pp. 638–641). Karl Marx (1996, pp. 84–85) observed our exchange of products and pointed out that we are not aware of what we are doing (namely, equating different kinds of human labor) by equating the products. He found latency in the dimension of social interaction, or systems-theoretically communicative operation. Observation creates two latencies: that which is not observed and the observation itself. The "operational latency" also appears in the mass media's observation (Luhmann, 1994). Journalists may not reflect on what they excluded from the spotlight and how they select and frame their news materials because they are wholly involved in the daily reproduction of news reports. However, as we see in studies of news values and media frames, the functionally differentiated society provides second-order observation of journalism.

---

17   For further on these points, see Esposito (2022). An avant-garde art movement in Japan wants to see art created by machines (Artificial Intelligence Art and Aesthetics Research Group, 2019). The machines' art, which organizes its production in accordance with machines' aesthetics, is regarded as non-human art per se.

There are always latencies, or sociocybernetically blind spots, and second-order observations that intend to reveal them. The chasing cycle constitutes a fundamental condition of meaning construction. The inevitable and constant reproduction of latencies is worth sociological attention. However, we may look at other aspects of the problem of eigenvalue formation. Reality appears to be accepted when unchallenged because of some social conditions, such as public apathy, political stalemate, and unmanageable societal complexity. This means that the plausibility of meaning may have multiple social backgrounds that should be treated intensively, especially in case-based studies.

Semantics provides understandability and acceptability in communication. It makes communication predictable enough for daily conversation. Semantics is not a frozen stock of meanings. It comes into play in actual flow of communication. This point leads us to the theory of sociocultural evolution, which defines the recursive process of societal selection of meaning. Luhmann discusses three mechanisms working in sociocultural evolution: *variation, selection,* and *restabilization* (Luhmann, 2012, pp. 251–336). Variation emerges as communication that is deviant from existing social expectations. We should note that deviance happens when something socially expected as known or normal is contradicted in communication. Deviance needs social standards such as norms and common knowledge from which it moves away. It is always embedded in a particular social situation. An idea that appears as a deviation will be accepted or rejected in subsequent communication. Deviance sometimes leads to *conflict* when it comes with saying "no" to ideas strongly supported or embraced by a group of people. Society has been developing procedures to regulate conflict in order to avoid violence, and such procedures enhance society's capacity to include variation within. Ideas and facts are selected when they are evident, convincing, or relevant to society. Functional systems and fundamental values give them chances to be accepted and have societal relevance. For instance, research findings obtained through proper scientific procedures will be accepted in the scientific community and become part of its common knowledge. An investigative report of human rights violations based on reliable sources will be newsworthy for journalism and update the public's perception of society. Those findings and facts should be accepted and discussed in other societal spheres, such as education and politics. This means that a group of systems handles variation and conducts selection in society (co-evolution or "mutual shaping") (Leydesdorff, 1994, 2021). After the publication of ideas and facts, second-order observations decide their destinies. Some new ideas referred to and repeatedly applied in subsequent communication may become part of society's repertoire of available meanings.

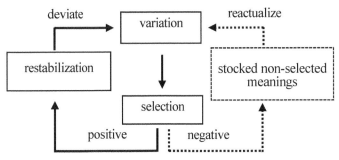

FIGURE 6   Cyclic process of meaning selection

Others will slip out of the public's attention but be stored in human memory, libraries, and databases. Selected meanings can enjoy temporary relevance and plausibility. However, new developments in society will, sooner or later, make those meanings out of date. Some meanings survive longer than others through their stabilization, such as normativization and dogmatization. The stabilization prepares updated standards for deviance, which triggers another selection of deviated meanings. In this respect, stabilization is always *resta*-bilization. Figure 6 shows the whole picture of the cyclic process of meaning selection.

Through the communicative process of sociocultural evolution, society shapes its expectational structures about what is right, what is normal, and what is true.[18] Variation occurs as deviation from stabilized meanings. Some meanings are accepted as evident, convincing, or socially relevant and become part of social expectations. Unaccepted meanings are archived in the social storage and will stay latent until they have occasion for reactualization. Sometimes variation may come with a new idea that has not been presented before. Society may also rediscover valuable ideas in the societal archive of meanings. It stores available meanings both in its expectational structure and the stock of latent meanings. We may discuss this ongoing selective actualization and deactualization of meanings as *social memory*, or organized access to meanings in social systems (Esposito, 2002).

---

18   Leydesdorff (2021) discusses meanings and expectations as central features involved in cultural evolution. John Mingers (2001) notes that social structure enables and restricts communication, and he mentioned the possibility of synthesizing Luhmann's concept of social structure as expectation and Gidden's view of structure. Leydesdorff (2010) combines Luhmann's social systems theory and Giddens' theory of structuration into a theory of structuration of expectations.

Luhmann (2012, p. 248) thought that we might call outcomes of combined effects of all the communication media (language, dissemination media, and the symbolically generalized media) "culture." An idea gradually becomes recognizable and reusable in different contexts through reiterated use and mention in communication. The tempo of cultural formation should be much slower than the attention cycle of news coverage. In the twentieth century, which saw the unprecedented development of media and information technologies, some ideas and visions have become the heritage of our time. From George Orwell's *1984* to Philip K. Dick's novels, for example, a variety of content has been adapted and reinterpreted. New and old heritage of meaning constitutes the stock of interpretive resources for the content industry and user-generated content. Each reinterpretation is made in combined contexts of economic, political, and various social situations. Walter Benjamin (2008) argued that film had liquidated "the value of tradition in the cultural heritage." Radical modern art offers plenty of examples that disturb the ordinary reproduction of meanings. It does not hesitate to be "infected" with mass culture, consumerism, new technology, and even political movements to introduce "Otherness" and become outsiders to the established styles of art (Groys, 2018, p. 72). Scholars found that trending topics on Twitter, a highly competitive arena for attention, were changing quickly (Kwak et al., 2010; Asur et al., 2011). Most memes, which went viral on social media, become part of the stockpile of reusable meanings on the web. However, as Umberto Eco (2006) wrote, culture is not just the stock of meanings. Rather it is the result of the never-ending process of selection.

Media of dissemination constitute decisively important conditions for exchanging and accumulating ideas expressed in communication. As Marshall McLuhan (1964) discussed, media extend our capability to communicate beyond distance and time. Luhmann repeatedly mentioned the historical impact of enhanced comparability introduced by writing and the printing press. "The possibilities for comparison also grew. Different books could be put side by side and read almost at the same time. This brought new intransparency" (Luhmann, 2012, p. 328). Today, we have far more comparability than we had in the era of the "Gutenberg Galaxy." In the contemporary communication environment, we can easily find different, often conflicting points of view and information (I will return to this point in 4.2). We are not sure whether we can reach a consensus even on the smallest issues in daily life. The "intransparency" may also involve "public anxiety, nervousness, irritability, discontent or strain," and tensions in society can be utilized for political purposes (Lasswell, 2013, p. 190). However, society does not fall apart at a single blow of political agitation and may instead show its resilience against challenges from the inside and outside.

1.3   *Problem-Solving as a Social Catalyst*

Practical efforts for problem-solving in our communities offer us grounded opportunities for the social construction of meaning. We are facing collective problems at all levels of society, that is, at global, national, and local levels. However, as "problems are the factually effective catalytic agents of social life" (Luhmann, 1995, p. 122), social systems theory finds here opportunities to start and organize communicative processes to deal with them. Anything that motivates people to act to make a difference in society can work as a social catalyst. But it may not remain after a series of processes devoted to a solution. In this respect, a problem as a social catalyst can be formulated as a social mediator, which vanishes after successful efforts.[19] A problem calls for action, and action leads to its result and lesson. People may discover their preferences through the learning process (Cohen et al., 1972, p. 1).

Unlike catalysts in chemical reactions, social problems are products of social construction through communicative processes.[20] Setting a problem properly is crucial for problem-solving. We try to remove something harmful and sometimes create a new opportunity in our social life. Generally, social movements set collective goals to make things better. From the viewpoint of this book, it is interesting that success of a social movement depends on effective use and contribution of media. When demonstrations and public gatherings are planned, they are expected to be reported by journalists. Social movements advocate that there is a problem that should be tackled and someone responsible for it. This is an effort to set a collective agenda and an initial phase of the societal process for problem-solving.

The societal process for problem-solving includes not only advocacy but also more direct action to improve situations. People voluntarily engage in rescue and recovery work in emergent situations after natural disasters such as earthquakes, cyclones/hurricanes/typhoons, and volcanic eruptions. One day after an earthquake hit southern Italy in 1980, a young guy opened a small coffee shop and gave free coffee to victims and people working there. As the demand and need for help grew, a small team was spontaneously organized around the coffee shop. But, on the third day, no one was there because the Army militarized the area (Lanzara, 1983, pp. 75–76). Giovan F. Lanzara (1983) discussed short-term, non-institutionalized units in extreme environments under his term "ephemeral organizations." In March 2011, in the wake of a

---

19   Based on Max Weber's intensive study of modern capitalism, Fredric Jameson (1973) formulated a catalytic agent of historical change as a "vanishing mediator." An advantage of this concept is to avoid causal explanations of history and keep focused on the unique roles of ideas in history.

20   For the implication of a chemical catalytic model, the Brusselator for sociocybernetics, see Laszlo (1986); Geyer (1995, pp. 123–124).

tsunami that devastated the northern Pacific coast of Japan's main island, a husband who lost contact with his wife drove to her workplace, a public high school, and found that hundreds of evacuees were stranded there without any help. As the tsunami had totally destroyed the town hall, the evacuees could not contact the municipal government. The husband and teachers agreed they needed to ask for help outside the town. Then, the husband became a messenger to a neighboring city (Takahashi, 2020, p. 38). This "improvised disaster response" (Lindell et al., 2007, pp. 160–161) by the people who cooperated in the disaster-hit area is another example of voluntary action to cope with collective problems. The short life of the coffee shop tells us of the fragility of such voluntary efforts. But they can be an essential part of social resilience. Georg Simmel underlined the importance of a multitude of interactions for "the toughness and elasticity … of social life" (Simmel, 1950, p. 10). Besides, we should note that people's activities are intertwined with other faces of self-organization in society, like politics and the mass media. These two processes of societal self-organization are observing and conditioning each other, and the interrelation constitutes the societal condition of meaning construction through problem-solving.

1.4   *Governing in a Complex Society*
The next point should be societal conditions of problem-solving in a complex society. What does "complex" mean in this context? Here it is worth visiting governance studies that have been refining the terminology to describe collective efforts. Jan Kooiman (2003, pp. 17–19) discussed three concepts that characterize conditions for governance in contemporary society: *diversity*, *dynamics*, and *complexity*.

Diversity refers to the condition of governing situations and actors. Kooiman drew a sociocybernetic implication of diversity for governance from W. Ross Ashby's (1968, p. 135) famous formulation, "only variety can destroy variety." He suggested that only a variety of actors can govern diverse situations. Current social issues such as gender policies and environmental protection increased the need for diverse expertise and international cooperation. This trend undermines a statist model, which regards state as a central and most powerful actor in governance. A networking model is considered for describing and organizing more flexible and diversified collaboration (Pierre & Peters, 2005). "These increasing complexities also require new sources of expertise, something which makes government more dependent on external sources of knowledge. The new governance could be seen as a way for the state to develop more continuous exchanges with such sources of expertise and knowledge" (Pierre & Peters, 2000, p. 66). *Dynamics* describes a tension between an actor's intention and social structure that sets a range of possible actions. When the existing legal system becomes an obstacle to an actor's activity, there should be tension between the actor's intention and the social structure. This tension will result in either replanning the activity or demanding a legal revision. Such tension and contradiction reflect societal dynamics. In the real world, diverse individual and collective actors are working on various issues with different intentions and geographical scopes. Some actors may collaborate, but others may compete for resources and social standings and even pursue conflicting goals. We cannot comprehend the whole situation and predict the trajectories of those efforts. This is the complexity of a pluralist society, where diverse agencies work simultaneously. Governing actors take part in this *complex* situation in order to make a difference.

Kooiman (2003, p. 4) defines our practical efforts to cope with collective problems and create a new opportunity as *"governing."* He distinguishes three different orders of governing (Kooiman, 2003, pp. 135, 153–156, 170–171). *The first order of governing* describes direct efforts for problem-solving and opportunity creation. People prepare a local festival, participate in cleaning-up activities after natural disasters, and discuss their requests to local governments. But, sometimes, we need to rethink our procedures and frameworks for governing and rebuild them to adapt to changing situations. This reflexive effort belongs to *the second order of governing*. It includes building a new framework, such as public-private cooperation for tackling problems in a local community or international collaboration for global warming control. If we intend to receive positive resonance and support from society, our causes must be justified by norms and values shared by fellow citizens. This type of governing is *the third order of governing*, also called "meta-governance."

In a diverse and changing society, meta-governance may involve tensions between people over acceptable norms and values, and some tensions could lead to conflicts in society. Governing efforts to cope with those tensions demand tolerance and time. Living with tensions over norms and values has been and will be one of the most critical challenges in a *diverse, dynamic*, and *complex* society. A serious problem appears when a conflict intensifies and agitators successfully persuade people to be intolerant of those who do not share their perspective and even see them as "enemies." This can trigger a vicious spiral that seriously damages social stability and mutual trust among fellow citizens (see 3.3 and 3.4 for the problem of conflict).

We can see a dazzling variety of governing actors working locally and globally. However, they are not in harmony with each other like an ideal organism. The whole picture is rather close to "organized anarchies" that include inconsistent preferences, trial-and-error, and fluid participation (Cohen et al., 1972, p. 1).

Being fraught with tensions and discord, governing efforts as a whole constitute the governance of society. I will call it *societal governance* (Kooiman, 2003; Takahashi, 2015b). Societal governance is as diverse, dynamic, and complex as society itself. It also includes the social construction of meaning through discussing goals and practicing values. Some of them may be embraced by relatively small groups. But others may be discussed on more open communication platforms like the press and social media. Therefore, we cannot think about the societal process of problem-solving without considering the contemporary communication environment and news circulation. Every collective goal must be advocated through the media if it seeks understanding and support from fellow citizens. Journalists have been the first and most powerful reporters of collective concerns from the beginning of the era of the mass media. In the next part, I will discuss the function of the mass media and the societal role of journalism from the perspective of social systems theory.

Part 2: Media, Journalism, and Society

2.1 *Journalism and News Values*

In 1910, Max Weber argued that the study of the newspaper was an urgent task for sociology. He raised two interesting questions. The first is about how the newspaper shapes the characteristics of people, and the second is about its effects on people's beliefs and knowledge (Weber, 2016, p. 274). Weber, famous for his intensive study of religious ideas that mediated Western society's historical transformation into modernity, suggested that journalism had become a major player in the social construction of meaning. The experience of World War I heightened the awareness that public opinion is not a spontaneous expression of people's feelings and opinions but a product of interventions. In his book *Public Opinion* (first published in 1922), Lippmann wrote that people's thinking had become more malleable than before. "Within the life of the generation now in control of affairs, persuasion has become a self-conscious art and a regular organ of popular government. … Under the impact of propaganda, … the old constants of our thinking have become variables. It is no longer possible, for example, to believe in the original dogma of democracy; that the knowledge needed for the management of human affairs comes up spontaneously from the human heart" (Lippmann, 2018, p. 109). Whereas Lippman thought that propaganda implies some sort of censorship that hinders the public from knowing facts and opinions, Edward L. Bernays, one of the earliest experts on propaganda and public relations in the twentieth century, gave a different view. "Mr. Lippmann says propaganda is dependent upon censorship. From my point of view the precise reverse is more nearly true. Propaganda is a purposeful, directed effort to overcome censorship – the censorship of the group mind and the herd reaction" (Bernays, 1961, p. 122). For Bernays, individual or collective stereotyped thinking was a censoring mechanism that must be removed or bypassed by propaganda. "The average citizen is the world's most efficient censor. His own mind is the greatest barrier between him and the facts" (Bernays, 1961, p. 122). It is surprising from today's perspective that "propaganda," in Bernays' view, was a messaging technique for those who were responsible for guiding people to the right path (Bernays, 1928, p. 159, 1961, pp. 217–218).[21]

Bernays saw that the nature of journalism is pursuing news values. "Today the leading editorial offices take the view that the real criterion governing the publication or non-publication of matter which comes to the desk is its news value" (Bernays, 1928, p. 151). Fundamentally, news subjects must be relevant to news outlets' audiences and facts must be acquired from reliable sources. Every piece of information, including propagandist ones, must fulfill the basic criteria and some news values in order to be news. Lippmann likened journalism to a social searchlight working day and night and drawing public attention to collective issues (Lippmann, 2018, p. 156). This metaphor also implies that journalism inevitably puts some episodes in the light and others in the dark. This means that each news article is a result of a series of selections in the news production process. Kurt Lewin's (1943; 1947) model of food circulation channels offered another metaphor for journalism. Citing Lewin's study, scholars formulated journalists as "gatekeepers" of news production (Shoemaker & Vos, 2009).

Both metaphors share a perception of inevitable selectivity in news production. John Zaller (2003) defined two standards of news coverage: the *Full News* standard and the *Burglar Alarm* standard. Whereas the *Full News* standard intends to cover public affairs comprehensively, the *Burglar Alarm* standard focuses on "matters requiring urgent attention" from the public (Zaller, 2003, pp. 114,122). Amber E. Boydstun (2013, pp. 6–7) reformulated the distinction and defined *patrol* and *alarm* models. The former describes the role of journalism as a societal "watchdog" that surveys every part of society for public issues.

---

21   During World War I, Bernays worked for the first American propaganda agency (the *Committee on Public Information*, also known as the *Creel Committee*). He headed a section that distributed texts and photographs expressing American views to countries of Latin America and later Europe (Manning, 2004, p. 24; Creel, 2015, p. 266). In 1937, he attended a meeting held in Boston that prepared the launch of the *Institute for Propaganda Analysis* (see also *Introduction*), but it seems he was not impressed by the meeting (Sproule, 1997, p. 130).

This model is especially interested in journalism's fundamental role in democracy. The public receives a comprehensive briefing from journalists every day and occasionally makes their decisions as voters. Bill Kovach and Tom Rosenstiel (2021, p. 7) write that providing information for citizens' freedom and self-governing is the primary purpose of journalism. These perspectives have a normative and ideal conception of journalism in democratic civil society. The latter model thinks journalism should inform the public about what requires urgent attention. According to this model, journalism neither can nor should cover all public affairs. "Journalists cannot talk about every potential problem because their audience would ignore them; it is the job of reporters ... to decide what requires attention and bring it to the public" (Zaller, 2003, p. 121). The public, facing the flood of information, does not and cannot pay attention to every news article, even if they have some importance. The alarm model just recommends journalists to be good gatekeepers.

Given that journalists are societal gatekeepers, the next problem is what criteria they use to find newsworthiness. News value studies provide a good starting point regarding the criteria for news production. In their pioneering work, Johan Galtung and Mari H. Ruge (1965, pp. 70–71) listed a dozen criteria in Norwegian foreign news (Table 1, left column). They thought the more an event met the criteria, the more likely it would be reported. Once covered, the event would be accentuated in terms of applied criteria. Based on their analysis of British newspapers and reconsideration of Galtung and Ruge's news value set, Tony Harcup and Deirdre O'Neill (2001) laid out a contemporary and more general set of news values (Table 1, center column). In Harcup and O'Neill's list, we find a soft news factor like "entertainment" and an organizational factor like "newspaper agenda." However, both lists share similar factors, such as surprise (unexpectedness), relevance (meaningfulness), and reference to elites.

In 2016, Harcup and O'Neill updated their news value list and added five new factors: *exclusivity, conflict, audio-visuals, shareability, and drama* (Harcup & O'Neill, 2016). Today's news media are watching the trend of attention from online audiences. We can find the most-read and most-watched lists on their websites. Harcup and O'Neill discuss that now social media have unignorable impacts on news selection and added "shareability" to their updated list. Shareability means that news media take account of stories "that are thought likely to generate sharing and comments via Facebook, Twitter and other forms of social media" (Harcup & O'Neill, 2016, p. 13). What happens to the autonomy of journalism when newsrooms become so eager to pick shareable stories? "Drama" is also interesting in terms of both shareability and social-political framing. Human stories are popular topics both on social and news media. They are stories of emotional moments of joy, grief, and hope. Accidents, disasters, and conflicts offer stages on which they are expressed. Those stories can be contextualized explicitly or implicitly by ideologies or social-political frames. Contemporary propaganda analysis discusses those cases using the term "narrative." "Narrative is more than just a story. Rather, ... it is an explanation of events in line with an ideology, theory, or belief" (Laity, 2015, p. 24). Intentionally or unintentionally, narratives are circulating on the vast complex of media. If Max Weber were alive today, he would be quite interested in the massive media communication and its impact on people's beliefs and knowledge.

We also find an account of news selection criteria in social systems theory. In his mass media theory, Luhmann (2000a) discussed ten criteria (Table 1, right column). Luhmann's news value list shares some factors with the two lists mentioned above. Novelty means that a topic brings something new to society. And when something happens with novelty, it will also cause a surprise and a feeling of unexpectedness. Luhmann suggests that relevance needs a certain frame of reference, such as locality. If a reported event has some implications for the audience's community, it will be relevant and meaningful to the audience.

The most important point about these criteria is the autonomy of journalism. Journalism studies have been interested in the profession's independence in society. Its editorial independence from political power and other potential influencers like advertisers is a crucial point for the autonomy of journalism. As we have seen above, audiences' attention can be another powerful influencer

TABLE 1   Criteria of news selection

Galtung and Ruge (1965)	Harcup and O'Neill (2001)	Luhmann (2000a)
unexpectedness	surprise	novelty, e.g., surprise
frequency/ threshold, e.g., intensity	magnitude	quantities
meaningfulness (relevance)	relevance	local relevance
reference to persons	celebrity	interest in particular people
reference to elite people / elite nations	the power elite	expression of opinions
reference to something negative	bad news	norm violation, e.g., scandal
consonance with pre-image	good news	moral distinction
unambiguity	entertainment	conflicts
continuity	follow-ups	topicality
composition	newspaper agenda	organizations and routines

regardless of whether journalists serve good citizens or entertain news consumers. The perspective of social systems theory is directed more to the social
structural dimension of journalism. Luhmann (2000a) focused on the function
of the mass media in the functionally differentiated society. Journalism scholars also have been developing their systems theoretical framework to describe
journalism's autonomy and societal role.

2.2   Niklas Luhmann's Theory of the Mass Media

The media constitutes an essential condition for constructing and accumulating meanings. Luhmann discussed that *the function of the mass media* is to
generate familiar objects and constantly update them. "It is therefore incumbent upon the mass media in the first instance to generate familiarity and vary
it from moment to moment so that in the following communication one can
risk provoking either acceptance or rejection" (Luhmann, 2000a, p. 101). Here,
"familiarity" means that we can assume that people are already acquainted
with a reported topic. In other words, the function of the mass media is to
generate such socially shared reality and create opportunities to communicate about current events in society. As discussed in agenda-setting studies,
media coverage gives salience to particular issues and events. Some topics
come under the spotlight, and others stay unnoticed or drop from the media
attention. Insofar as the ongoing selection orients discourses on socially relevant issues, the mass media decide social memory (Esposito, 2002, 2016). "The
memory of our society ... is constituted first of all by the mass media and ruled
by their always changing forms, submitted to the iron law of the search for
novelty (news)" (Esposito, 2008, p. 188). The past and the future of society are
thematized or redescribed in the present context, which journalists define. In
this respect, journalism engages in historical descriptions of society.

Luhmann discussed the mass media in both technological and communicative dimensions. He defined the mass media as "all those institutions of society which make use of copying technologies to disseminate communication"
(Luhmann, 2000a, p. 2). Media of dissemination, such as the printing press
and digital media, are technological tools to secure the reachability of messages. The mass reachability is the technological foundation for producing
"familiarity" in society. Luhmann applied a key systems theoretical concept,
namely the distinction between system and environment, to the communicative dimension of the mass media. If mass communication is autonomous
in its self-reproduction, there must be a border between the system of mass
communication and its societal environment. Luhmann energetically offered
plenty of descriptions of functional systems, such as political, economic, legal,
and scientific systems. His theory of communication systems gives a common

framework to describe those systems' self-determination. "For function systems, and thus also in the case of the mass media, this typically occurs by means of a binary code which fixes a positive and a negative value" (Luhmann, 2000a, p. 16). Steering its operation by using a code, a system continuously makes its own choices about what is to be communicated or not. Luhmann defined the mass media's code at an abstract level. "The code of the system of the mass media is the distinction of information and non-information" (Luhmann, 2000a, p. 17). By this distinction, the mass media system steers its communicative process in three strands: *news and in-depth reporting (journalism)*, *advertisement*, and *entertainment*. The three strands have their programs to operate the code in concrete contexts, such as news values (journalism), the novelty of products and services (advertisement), and content that constructs fictional realities (entertainment). The system must constantly reproduce novelty – "the iron law"! – because information value decays as soon as it is communicated (Luhmann, 2000a, 2013, p. 262).

As seen in the previous section, a dozen news values work as news selection criteria for sorting out potential materials. Based on the criteria, journalism allocates positive and negative values of the code information/non-information to each reporting material. Put differently, journalism operates by processing newsworthiness. For society, journalism generates and disseminates *familiar* topics with novelty and societal relevance. We can bring those topics up in a conversation, assuming other people already know them. The mass media's selective dissemination of information brings about adaptive responses in other functional systems. Politicians observe news coverage and understand what people are informed about the current political scene, and would adjust their behavior to the perceived reality of their constituencies.

2.3   *Systems Theory of Journalism and the Public Sphere*

In journalism studies, scholars have been making efforts to construct social systems theories of journalism. After the pioneering work of Manfred Rühl (1969a, 1969b, 1980), the discussion on the societal role of journalism and its systems theoretical understanding was activated in the 1990s. Rühl (1980) hypothetically formulated that norms and criteria of the profession's practice somehow depend on the complexity level of society. A series of journalism theories identified journalism's societal function and described journalism as an autonomous subsystem of society. Bernd Blöbaum (1994) discussed that the modernization process in the eighteenth and nineteenth centuries prepared a societal condition for journalism. Society needs synchronization through public communication on socially relevant events and situations as it becomes more differentiated. "The journalism system takes over a function in society. The system offers its services to other social systems. Journalism distinguishes itself from society and other subsystems" (Blöbaum, 1994, p. 256, my translation). Siegfried Weischenberg (1994) formulated that a function of the social system of journalism in modern society is gathering the latest information from diverse subsystems of society and making it available everywhere. He used the onion model of journalism to elaborate on the societal function of journalism.[22] The onion model sees that the practice of journalism is a combined result of four different layers of factors, such as (1) historical, legal basis and the profession's ethical standards, (2) economic, political, organizational, and technological imperatives, (3) information sources and styles of reporting, (4) social and political attitudes and self-understanding of the profession.

Alexander Görke and Matthias Kohring (1996, p. 17) argued that the border of the journalism system should be built with meaning created through communication. This perspective led them to their critical reception of Luhmann's (2000a) theory of the mass media. Luhmann defined the mass media in terms of their technological function in society and also discussed the *communication system* of the mass media. The scholars argued that journalism theory should focus on the communicative dimension of journalism (Kohring & Hug, 1997, p. 31). This perspective is related to their theoretical framework. Whereas the theories discussed in the first half of the 1990s observed journalism as an autonomous social system that can be distinguished from other subsystems of society (Blöbaum, 1994; Weischenberg, 1994), Kohring, Görke, and Detlef M. Hug formulated journalism as a subsystem of the public sphere. "We regard ... that not journalism itself but the public sphere as a functional system" (Kohring & Hug, 1997, p. 31, my translation).

The theory of the public sphere system thinks that the system appeared in response to a historical circumstance that demands continuous observation of society and public communication. "In a functionally differentiated society characterized by its diversity of observers' perspectives, *continuous observation of events* must be *maintained to build mutual expectations on the environment*. ... Society responds to this problem by differentiating its own functional system. We call this functional system *public sphere*" (Kohring, 1997, p. 248, my translation, emphasis in the original). These journalism scholars have a common understanding of the characteristic of modern society: functional differentiation. As stated above (Introduction), functional differentiation is the structural condition of the incongruity, or the diversity of perspectives

---

22   For the onion model, see also Weischenberg (1990, 2004) and Scholl and Weischenberg (1998). Stephen D. Reese and Shoemaker (2016) distinguish five layers of analysis (society, institution, organization, routine, individual) in their hierarchy of influences model.

between societal subsystems and, therefore, the complexity of modern society. The societal condition has created a demand for observing society and sharing updated information about public issues. Görke (2003, p. 128) observes that the demand for societal *synchronization* has grown under functional differentiation. Social systems build their expectational structures, which determine systems' sensitivity to irritation from the outside. Through structure-building, systems become autonomous in processing information, but the autonomy risks being insensitive to the societal environment. This insensitivity can be criticized by external observers. Public discourse on the latest and socially relevant issues may disturb systems' usual ways of operation. For instance, "the striving for power" (Weber, 2008, p. 194) sometimes causes a political scandal or stalemate. It may drive everything inside the political world. However, politicians cannot ignore the public's attention. When a political scandal comes to light, the political system is exposed to external observations and urged to reconsider its manner of operation under public scrutiny.

Here arises a question: How does the public sphere system build its communicative border in society? The journalism scholars discussed a binary code with which the public sphere communicatively closes itself from its societal environment. Hug (1997, p. 331) formulated the code of the public sphere as *relevant-to-environment/not-relevant-to-environment*. Reflecting on the multipolar structure of the functionally differentiated society, Kohring (1997, pp. 249–251, 2006, p. 168) identified the code as *multiple-systems-relevant/ not-multiple-systems-relevant*.[23] A multiple-systems-relevant event can be contextualized in more than one particular system and facilitates subsequent communication in multiple systems. In this respect, the event has societal relevance. These concepts tell that detecting socially relevant events and information is crucial to the public sphere system. If politicians' unnecessary power struggles result in parliamentary and governmental dysfunction, that will raise serious concerns in every quarter of society. Usually, scientific research remains out of the attention of the public. But some innovative research can be relevant to policymakers, related industries, and consumers. The public sphere is considered to be comprised of communication on such socially relevant topics. Görke (1999, pp. 310–316) thought that the public sphere's code must be able to handle the temporal dimension of information. He termed the code *actuality* to indicate the novelty and temporality of information relevant to

---

23   In German, Kohring's code is formulated as *mehrsystemzugehörig/nicht-mehrsystem-zugehörig*. The distinction mentions that it is important to the public sphere system whether a topic belongs to multiple systems or not. Here I understand, with Dennis Nguyen (2017), that the code is used to see whether a topic is relevant to multiple systems.

the public sphere. The code also reflects the temporality of societal synchro-nization through communicating *actual* issues. As we see that headlines and trending topics are changing from moment to moment, societal synchroniza-tion inevitably has a transient nature. These public sphere theories describe that the system organizes itself with its own code and assumes a societal role. Then, our question moves to the relationship between the public sphere and journalism.

The public sphere theorists observe that journalism plays a key role in per-forming the societal function of the public sphere (Kohring, 1997, p. 251, 2006, p. 159, 2016, p. 172). "The differentiation of journalism, that is the professional-ization of journalistic practice, formation of communicative style particular to journalism, the establishment of social organizations as editorial office ... are necessary conditions of communicative reproduction in the public sphere system" (Hug, 1997, pp. 335–336, my translation). In this framework, the jour-nalism system is not identified with the system of the public sphere. The latter also includes communicative activities of non-journalistic participants. Both civic advocates and journalists can call for public attention to public affairs and related social policies. The second half of the 1990s, when these theo-ries appeared, saw the early development in the number of individuals using the Internet (Figure 7). In this early stage of the Internet era, Robert Kraut and his colleagues found the "Internet paradox" between greater use of the Internet and a decline in the size of users' social circle (Kraut et al., 1998). For Jürgen Habermas, a leading scholar in the debate on the public sphere, the consequences of the Internet were still unclear. In 1998 he wrote, "The men-tal fall-out of the Internet ... is as yet hard to assess" (Habermas, 1998, p. 310).

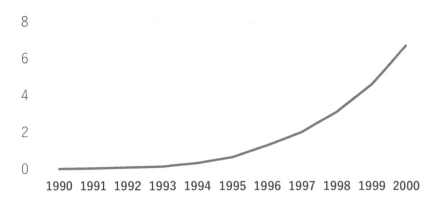

FIGURE 7   Individuals using the Internet, 1990–2000 (% of population, World)
SOURCE: INTERNATIONAL TELECOMMUNICATION UNION (ITU) WORLD
TELECOMMUNICATION/ICT INDICATORS DATABASE, THE WORLD BANK

However, Kraut and his colleagues' follow-up research conducted in the late 1990s showed that using the Internet was associated with an increase in the size of social circles and involvement in community activities (Kraut et al., 2002). As the Internet's potential for building *online communities* and organizing civic activities was revealed, debates and studies on the relationship between computer-mediated communication and democracy were activated under the concept of "electronic democracy" (Ess, 1996; Friedland, 1996; Tsagarousianou, 2000) and "cyberdemocracy" (Tsagarousianou et al., 1998). What implications did the activated civic communication have for journalism's de facto monopoly in the public sphere?

The two-layered journalism theory fits the circumstances of media communication because – after the late 1990s – we can no longer think that journalism represents the public sphere, though it is still an essential part of it. Then, how does the communication system of journalism hold its autonomy in the public sphere? (Note that Luhmann identified journalism as a program strand of the mass media.) Kohring (2006, pp. 173–175) argues that *novelty* and *relevance* regulate the use of the public sphere's code (multi-systems-relevant/not-multi-systems-relevant) as *programs* in journalism. In order to decide the allocation of positive and negative values of the code, journalism has to develop its understanding of what is new and relevant to societal subsystems and the public. Otherwise, journalism cannot perform a key role in the public sphere. This condition makes applications of its programs more dependent on the perception of the societal environment than other functional systems like science. Görke (1999, p. 301) finds the difference between journalism and the public sphere in the complexity level. By definition, the communication system of the public sphere includes whole conversations on *actual* topics in society. However, news reports are products of a series of editorial selections. When we complain that media outlets do not cover what interests us, we observe a gap in the complexity level between the public sphere and journalism. As the alarm model says, reporters do not intend to cover everything relevant to society. So, journalism has to prepare its programs, which steer the selectivity of reporting. Görke (1999, p. 322) agrees that the structures of journalism, such as news values and its self-defined role, become more complex along with the complexity of society (Rühl, 1980, p. 259). This insight suggests that journalism's programs reflect the complexity level of the time and we can read it from changes and invention of news values. He observes that the scope of *personalization*, which is to focus on newsworthy persons and construct news reports as stories of those people, has expanded from a handful of elites to every kind of celebrity and ordinary people who have socially relevant experiences (Görke, 1999, pp. 322–323). For researchers interested in historical studies of journalism, the studies of news values and the efforts of redefining the profession's societal role (see 5.1, 5.2) offer materials for reconsidering journalism in the modern complex society.

2.4   The Public Sphere and Journalistic Autonomy

The systems theories of journalism and the public sphere focus on the communicative dimension of those two systems. Their framework notes that the public sphere only partially depends on the media, like printing and broadcasting technologies. This means that the public sphere also includes an enormous number of non-mediated communication. Then, how does journalism organize its communicative contribution in the sea of the public sphere? After the launches of powerful social media platforms in the 2000s, the power balance between journalists and non-journalistic information sources has become open to discussion (see 4.2). Harcup and O'Neill (2016) have added "shareability" to their news value list. Does this suggest that journalism has become more sensitive to the public's attention? Is journalistic autonomy melting down into the massive flow of online communication and its attention economy? Its news values, organizational routines, and the profession's ethics will continue to be deciding factors in daily news production. However, considering the contemporary communication environment and the growing political pressure on journalism, its autonomy should be an important issue that needs careful observation.

A sociological theory of social systems offered a different perception of the nature of the public sphere. Dirk Baecker (1996) formulated the public sphere (Öffentlichkeit) as openness for second-order observation of systems' boundaries rather than a specific type of communication system. For Baecker, the public sphere operates as "boundary crossing" (Baecker, 1996, pp. 94–95, my translation). Using the distinction of system and environment, every system distinguishes itself from its environment. A system's operations actualize selected possibilities and make the others latent. However, an observer can *cross* the boundary and refer to the other side of the distinction: the system's environment. The observer can also recross the boundary and look at the system side again (Spencer-Brown, 2021). Through boundary crossing, an observer can see the inside and the outside of the system. Baecker discusses that every system is open for such second-order observation. "The public sphere is an operation of 'opening'" (Baecker, 1996, p. 95, my translation).[24] We can observe what is and is not reported by journalists, and both audiences and journalists

---

24   Based on Baecker's definition of the public sphere, Luhmann (2000a) discussed it as a
      medium of reflexive observation of systems' boundaries in society.

can conduct the second-order observation of news reporting. In a society where "'everybody' observes everybody else" (Shoemaker & Reese, 2014, p. 180) and talks about what they observed, every communication system could be a subject of second-order observation. This is a fundamental condition of an open society. The openness for second-order observation brings about a risk of undermining systems' stability and an opportunity to reconsider conventional patterns of communication. In Görke's terminology, openness is indispensable for societal "synchronization" and journalism's contribution to society.

In the case of the mass media, especially journalism, as news production is always a result of editorial selections, journalism reproduces the distinction between what is reported and not reported. The former increases its salience for the public; the latter remains in the shadow of public attention. However, "the trouble lies deeper than the press" (Lippmann, 2018, p. 156). The public can pay attention to and talk about non-salient issues if necessary. Therefore, the system of the mass media is reproducing a "form" in Spencer-Brown's (2021) sense by producing "marked" and "unmarked" issues in society. Today, countless observations are publicly expressed and ready to be subjects of second-order observation, which stimulates further communication. The massive flow of communication about first- and second-order observation has become more visible in this Internet era.

Most observations presented as written or spoken messages find only a small number of readers and listeners. They will be simply forgotten as soon as communicated. Lack of time prevents us from reading and listening carefully. However, some messages catch the public's attention and trigger further communicative reactions. In order to describe the selective factors of information processing, the concept of "schema," a chunk of knowledge that tells people what is interesting and how things can be understood, has been discussed in media studies. Graber (1984, p. 24) formulated four major functions of schemas that work at the personal and cognitive level: (1) to determine what information will be processed, (2) to help in processing information within an existing framework of understanding, (3) to make it possible to understand things even when people are not provided with adequate information, (4) to help in solving problems by giving additional information. People form schemas that include knowledge about "familiar causal sequences" and "typical human behavior" based on their life experiences. Graber found that people, using their schemas, predict outcomes of current situations, judge whether a person can be trusted, and find stories they can empathize with (Graber, 1984, pp. 155–166, 171–173).

At the collective and communicative level, morality is also important because it provides a set of criteria for judging persons' behaviors and their consequences. People are familiar with the moral code that distinguishes between good and bad behaviors and respectable and disrespectable persons (Luhmann, 2012, p. 239). Görke (1999, pp. 325–327) identified the moral distinction between good and bad as a programmatic distinction for the journalistic code (*actuality*). Luhmann also mentioned it as a criterion of news selection (see Table 1). Politicians' undesirable behaviors often appear in headlines and stir up people's interest on social media. Morality is serving the primary code of the systems striving for something *actual* or *informative*. However, this does not mean that journalism contributes to building a common and standard moral code. "The mass media merely provide a constant irritation for society, a reproduction of moral sensitivity" (Luhmann, 2000a, p. 31). People may or may not agree with a moral judgment suggested by a news article. A news report which includes a moral judgment stimulates further moral observation and communication, possibly contradicting each other.

Using morality as a news value raises the same question about journalistic autonomy as "shareability" does. The moral code belongs to society, the journalism system's societal environment. The more journalism uses the moral code in news production, the deeper the perspective of its environment penetrates its editing process. This does not immediately mean that journalism is not autonomous or "allopoietic" in society. Regardless of whether it is morally desirable, each functional system is inclined to operate stubbornly. Power struggles and their will to survive in the political world sometimes make politicians blind to public interest and morality. Graber (1984, p. 163) reported that when her panelists talked about politicians' misbehavior, they repeatedly said, "I expect something like that … I just take it sort of matter of fact that that's what politicians do." Scientific research is conducted taking account of research contexts. So, scholars do not always make research plans to serve the public. Artists sometimes venture to irritate the ordinary sense of beauty and morality. We may find such stubbornness in journalists' brave investigations of fact and media frenzy. However, we have to examine journalism's interrelation with its societal environment.

Part 3: Media and Politics

3.1 *Politics and the Mass Media*

This part extends our scope by involving another societal domain in our consideration of the mass media and journalism. In the era of television, well-performing on the screen of the mass media became a crucial skill for politicians. Roger Ailes, the founder of Fox News, recalled that in 1967 he said to Richard Nixon that campaigning on television is not a political "gimmick,"

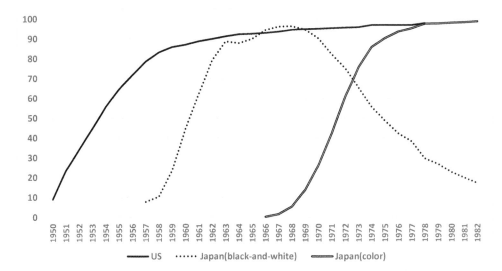

FIGURE 8   Television holders, 1950–1982 (% of household, US and Japan)
SOURCE: STEINBERG (1982), CONSUMER CONFIDENCE SURVEY (THE CABINET OFFICE
OF JAPAN)

rather television is "the most powerful means of communication ever devised
by man" and "nobody would ever be elected to major office again without
presenting himself reasonably well on TV" (Diamond & Bates, 1992, p. 149).
In the 1950s, television sets spread rapidly in the households of the United
States. Other countries like Japan were catching up at the same rapid pace in
the late 1950s. According to the statistics in Japan, color television replaced
black-and-white television in the early 1970s (Figure 8).

Looking back at the early stage of the television era, Dwight D. Eisenhower,
sitting in a film studio for his campaign spots in 1952, said, "to think that an old
soldier should come to this!" (Diamond & Bates, 1992, p. 55). However, eight
years after his remark, the presidential debate between Kennedy and Nixon
in 1960 showed that visual images on television had an unignorable impact
on the campaign (Dodds & Rozell, 2000, p. 152). In the 1980s, Ronald Reagan
presented one of the most prominent cases of "television presidency" (Cronin,
1980, p. 100). The characteristic of Reagan's "primetime presidency" is that his
messages, behavior, and even his persona were crafted to fit presenting himself
on the screen of television (Denton, 1988, p. xii). In 1984, CBS News delivered a
critical report of Reagan's presidency full of his visual images in various events
and ceremonies. Leslie Stahl, the reporter of the program, critically described
how the Reagan administration utilized visual images to create and protect
his popularity. She thought that officials in the White House did not like her

report. But an official said to her that they enjoyed the report as a "free ad for the Ronald Reagan campaign for reelection" (Davis, 2001, p. 156). Later, in 1989, she recalled this episode and said in a documentary program: "We just didn't get the enormity of the visual impact over the verbal."[25] If an image talks more than words, as Ailes said, politicians have to get used to and be skilled at appearing on television. "Thus, politics becomes an activity of style over substance, image over reality, melodrama over analysis, belief over knowing, awareness over understanding" (Denton, 1988, p. 24). However, this does not mean that politics has become a servant to news media. As the Reagan administration official said, a potential appeal of appearance on the television screen is interpreted and evaluated from a political point of view. Politicians are doing nothing but politics, just like journalists are doing their job.

In the 1990s, the transitional decade to the Internet era, the landscape of media and politics changed, involving new campaign strategies with new media such as cable television, fax machines, and email. Bill Clinton's communication team used faxes, emails, and other new communication tools to make a quick countercharge against negative information about him and found opportunities in television and radio talk shows to present his personality to voters (Myers, 1993). Ross Perot, the independent candidate for the U.S. presidency, announced his candidacy on Larry King Live, a talk and interview program on CNN. The "talk show campaign" undermined the influence of serious news programs on the presidential election and connected candidates to citizens more directly. The new campaign style was also a chance for soft-format programs to invite presidential candidates and catch the public's and even professional journalists' attention (Diamond et al., 1993).

Observing from the viewpoint of Luhmann's social systems theory, this section describes the interrelation between the mass media and politics (Figure 9). The communication system of the mass media is constantly observing politics. It operates with its binary code information/not information, more specifically, newsworthy/not newsworthy. News media of both hard and soft formats acquire news materials from the political world. News outlets report candidates' comments, the government's statements, and congressional resolutions. Sometimes political communication is staged on television in debate format programs. In both cases, the mass media contextualize its material in journalistic or entertaining frames. Luhmann describes politics as another autonomous functional system in society. In his framework, the communication system of politics operates with the binary code powerful/powerless.

---

25   See the transcript of "Illusions of News" broadcasted in 1989 by PBS (available at: https://billmoyers.com/content/illusions-news/).

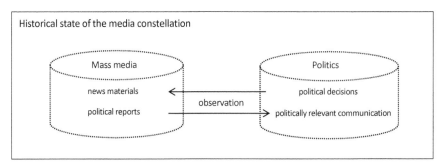

FIGURE 9   Interrelation between the mass media and politics

In the legislatures of democratic institutions, the political code works as the distinction between ruling parties and oppositions. The former, the positive side of the distinction, has an advantage in *preparing the capacity for making collectively binding decisions*, which is the societal function of the political system (Luhmann, 2000b, pp. 84–88). Like the mass media system, the political system observes the mass media and finds politically relevant communication, which stimulates further political communication. Politicians are watching news reports and TV programs on politics and recognizing how the people observe themselves and their rivals. These observations become premises for subsequent political decisions.

Since Maxwell E. McCombs and Donald L. Shaw (1972) discussed the mass media's function of agenda-setting, scholars have been interested in the mass media's power to sort out political issues and make some of them more salient in the audience's perception. Polls, officials' comments, and other exemplar opinions about salient topics appear in news articles and broadcasting programs. Through its second-order observation of how the people observe political issues and scenes, the political system sees itself in a "mirror" of public opinion (Luhmann, 1992). The social systems theory does not consider public opinion as individuals' attitudes or beliefs on public issues. Instead, the theory defines it as socially relevant themes. A salient political issue stimulates the public's communication. It contributes to forming a virtual opinion forum that reflects various views on the subject. This makes, to some extent, the distribution of opinions more visible for second-order observers. As every salient agenda is a product of a series of selections, there are always other agendas worth catching the public's attention. The visibility of alternative views helps the political system see and handle contingency over making a political decision (Luhmann, 1971b).

Importantly the function of public themes has a prerequisite in the communicative dimension. Luhmann (1971b, p. 13) distinguished two aspects of public communication: selecting themes and expressing opinions. These aspects must be separated in order to see social complexity, that is, changing socially relevant topics and individuals' views on them. In a free and democratic society, people can express their opinions on any topic. There, we can see a picture of a landscape or distribution map of expressed views in our minds. Politicians may find themselves in the landscape and think about how they behave in the communicative scene over publicly discussed agendas. In an authoritarian regime, public opinion cannot be a "mirror" for power elites. They do not want the public mirror which reflects them. They are keen to control agenda-setting and suppress politically undesirable voices using every trick in the book. This means they know that the mirror reflects what they do not want to see if no intervention is made. However, even in a democratic society, the mirror can be covered by a mist of silence. When a person talks about a morally right thing, addressees may feel they are expected to agree. Luhmann (1971b, p. 14) finds non-interactivity in such moral communication. Of course, an addressee might dare to express a different perspective, but those attending should prepare for a lengthy argument. Morality reduces the improbability of acceptance in communication. Still, it does not fit to make public opinion visible and contribute to second-order observation in society. In this respect, liberty as "the right to tell people what they do not want to hear" (Orwell, 2000, p. 107) should work better than morality.

3.2 Politics and Morality

In the seventeenth century, the early days of news media, politicians could avoid being watched and scrutinized by the public over their behavior. "The Lords and Commons considered it a breach of privilege to publish the debates or identify individual members by name and they insisted on this privilege until the 1770s" (Slauter, 2015, p. 27). Max Weber (2016, p. 264) mentioned that the situation had drastically changed by his time. As seen in the previous section, the communication systems of politics and the mass media interact very closely. This section discusses the interrelation of the two systems in terms of morality that characterizes a contemporary style of political communication.

After Ronald Reagan's "primetime presidency" presented a salient example of televised politics, and just before the dawn of the Internet age, political scientists noticed that a growing trend of a political phenomenon called "populism" was spreading in Western democracies. "Since the early 1990s in Western Europe, populist movements have achieved their best ever results in countries like France, Switzerland and Denmark and have entered national government for the first time in states such Italy, Austria and the Netherlands" (Albertazzi

& McDonnell, 2008, p. 2). Historically, we find early cases of populism in the late nineteenth century in the United States and Russia. Juan Perón's leadership in Argentina is often referred to as a mid-twentieth-century case. Each case of the political phenomenon can be characterized by its movement, leadership, idea, and style in a different combination (Taggart, 2000, pp. 5–6). The phenomenon manifested itself recurrently in different social-historical backgrounds. This has made it "elusive" for populism scholars (Laclau, 1977, p. 143; Taggart, 2002, p. 66). This section mainly focuses on its communicative style to think about a characteristic of contemporary political communication from a sociocybernetic perspective. Jan Jagers and Stefaan Walgrave (2007, p. 322) define populism as "a political communication style of political actors that refer to the people." There are two important points for analyzing a style of political communication. The first point is media strategy. Politicians try to maximize access to their constituencies and improve the public's recognition of their policies and personalities through the available media. The second point is message strategy. We could say that constructing a proper message in terms of when, what, to whom, and how is a critical skill for politicians. Also, in Machiavelli's time, acquiring esteem and not being hated by the people were more important than building a fortress (Machiavelli, 2005). In the cases of populism in recent decades, scholars find that referring to "the people" and their alleged enemy constitutes a fundamental scheme to organize political messages.

Observing a surge in support for far-right parties in Western Europe in the 1980s and 1990s, Paul Taggart (1995; 2000) termed the political phenomenon "new populism." He found its characteristics in "anti-institutional" politics, which attacks the existing political parties and party systems (Taggart, 2000, pp. 73–76). Margaret Canovan (2005, pp. 74–78) added another type of populism: "politicians' populism." In contrast to the former type, this type of populism is exemplified by exiting politicians recognized as members of the political establishment, like Tony Blair in the U.K. Dave Snow and Benjamin Moffitt (2012) also discussed this type and termed it "mainstream populism." Canovan pointed out that the media have more impact on forming this type of populist movement than social divisions based on class and ideology. "Television maximizes the importance of personal leadership, allowing and encouraging leaders to appeal to the electorate as a whole" (Canovan, 2005, p. 77). In the case of the U.S. presidential election in 1992, challengers utilized new media to fight against the incumbent candidate, who had more opportunities to enjoy media exposure. In the case of politicians' populism, existing politicians appeal to the people through the mass media. The media strategies adopted by the establishment and anti-establishment were different. However, both send their messages to a homogeneous group of addressees, or "'the people' understood as a single body with common interests" (Canovan, 2005, p. 78).[26]

Like every style of political struggle, populism sets a "we" and "they" distinction. Populists appeal that they are standing on the side of the people and confronting those who harm the interests of the people. The definition of populism proposed by Cas Mudde and Cristóbal Rovira Kaltwasser says that the distinction in contemporary populism brings politics into moral confrontation. They think that populism is a "thin-centred ideology that considers society to be ultimately separated into two homogeneous and antagonistic groups, 'the pure people' and 'the corrupt elite,' and which argues that politics should be an expression of the volonté générale (general will) of the people" (Mudde & Rovira Kaltwasser, 2012, p. 8). The pair of adjectives "pure" and "corrupt" indicates that morality matters most in the populists' schematization of political messages. The two scholars write "populism is in essence a form of *moral* politics" (Mudde & Rovira Kaltwasser, 2012, p. 8, emphasis in the original). Albertazzi and McDonnel (2008, p. 3) also find in populism moral confrontation between "virtuous" people and those who harm the people in various dimensions such as rights, values, and identity. Put differently, populists describe how 'the corrupt elite' caused a loss in "well-being" of the people and argue that they have a debt to be paid politically (Lakoff, 2016).

By "schematization," I mean defining A as B (see Luhmann, 2012, p. 61), for instance, labeling the establishment as the "corrupt elite" who are enjoying and protecting their vested interests. In this case, the schematization describes the establishment as morally bad and responsible for a loss in people's well-being. In the context of media studies, Graber (1984, p. 23) defined a *schema* as "a cognitive structure consisting of organized knowledge about situations and individuals." Schemas are formed through our daily experiences. As seen before (Introduction, 2.4), Graber tried to explain how people deal with the glut of information. Facing "flood tides of information through the mass media," people need to use the cognitive simplifying mechanism, which contains "general patterns" of things and human behavior and "prototypical examples" to understand them (Graber, 1984, pp. 23–24). Luhmann (2013, p. 321) thought schemas coordinate the processing of meaning between communication and consciousness "under highly complex, fast-changing conditions." Schemas can be updated and adopted flexibly along with the media and public attention cycle. A schema is more changeable and open for learning than language,

---

26   Canovan (2005, p. 78) finds a case that transited from the first type of populism to the second in Silvio Berlusconi's move in Italian politics.

which offers reusability of words and understandability in communication (Luhmann, 2012, p. 61). During the COVID-19 pandemic, wearing a mask in public spaces became a morally right thing. That should have been an unimaginable change in countries where wearing a mask was not a habit in daily life. I think that morality is one of the key schemas which is activated when people process information on politics and policies.[27] People may judge whether they can regard a politician as good, responsible, and trustworthy based on their moral standards. It does not need any expertise. Professionals like journalists can also make a moral judgment when they report politicians' misbehavior. As seen in populism studies, morality can be a political tool to win voters' support and put a rival in a socially difficult position.

We also find a case of "moral politics" in a non-Western country. Hideo Otake (2003, 2006) analyzed Prime Minister Junichiro Koizumi's political strategies in Japanese politics in the first half of the 2000s. He described Koizumi's political schematization that labeled his opponents as "resistance forces" who opposed his policy to revive the nation's economy and presented himself as a "reformer." Otake named Koizumi's political style a "reform populism." On the screen of the mass media, especially soft-format news programs on television, the political drama was quickly interpreted as a conflict between a "good" reformer fighting for the people's interest and the "bad" establishment. Interestingly, Koizumi became a "populist" as a result of the interrelation between politics and the mass media. He had been recognized as a non-mainstreamer because of his "eccentric" character and weak factional base within his party. However, this allowed him to gain remarkable popularity as a "reformer" through the mass media (Takahashi, 2015a).

Luhmann (2004, p. 167) distinguished *function* and *performance* of the functional systems in society. The former means its contribution to society at large. For instance, the societal function of the mass media is to create socially shared realities for daily communication. The latter concept describes outcomes of societal functions in other functional systems. We can observe the performance of the mass media system in its interrelation with politics. News reports on politics come out every day, and this is the usual business of journalism. The outcomes of news reporting appear in the political world but differently for each politician and party. Some may find opportunities, and others

---

27   George Lakoff (2016) described in detail some fundamental schemas that he found in the moral worldviews of conservatives and liberals in the United States, which often contradict each other, and argued that their moral reasoning is based on different ideal models of male and female parents (a *strict* father and *nurturant* mother). He discussed that these moral reasonings are deeply embedded in conservative and liberal ways of thinking.

may see risks in news coverage. This will stimulate further political communication and response in the mass media, such as a follow-up report. The interaction between politics and the mass media is always taking place. In the case of Japanese politics, it gave momentum to Koizumi's "reform populism."

If we distinguish the moral politics studied by populism scholars from a normal mode of democracy, our next question should be: What is the condition for populism to emerge in democracy? Understanding populism as a style of political performance, Moffitt and Simon Tormey (2014, pp. 391–394) mentioned its three elemental aspects. First, populists appeal to "the people," which is a core element of schematization in populism. Second, they intend to get political momentum from the people's perception of crisis, breakdown, or threat. Third, they tend to disregard the "appropriate" ways of behavior as politicians and present themselves as "outsiders" in the existing political world. We can combine these elements and trace a narrative of populism. The innocent people are suffering in a crisis that the establishment cannot resolve or even worsens; Only a political outsider can stand on the people's side and deal with the problem. In the narrative of populism, we see that appealing to a "sense of crisis" (Taggart, 2000, p. 5) or other extraordinary situations is utilized as leverage to set up a political climate in which populists' schematization works.

The notion of "crisis" is another schema that works in public opinion (Luhmann, 2000b, pp. 299–300). This schema describes a situation as almost unresolvable in terms of its scale and cost. Importantly the amplified seriousness makes it possible to allege that the problem is relevant to everyone. This increases the leverage in the political climate. In the context of political communication, political challengers can criticize those who are responsible and to blame for the "crisis" and intend to receive the public's support for their causes. The more a reason becomes broadly accepted, the more it will get enhanced in terms of social conformity and morality. John Locke (2000, pp. 252–261) discussed "the law of opinion or reputation" along with other categories of law (the law of God, the civil law). He writes that the law whereby people judge "virtue" and "vice" is enforced with commendation and discredit among fellow members of society or those of one's reference group. What implications does this have for political struggles? Those who successfully discredit political rivals can boost their political clout. Especially in a "crisis" situation, tackling the problem, whatever it is, should be regarded as the right thing. The urgent need for action is likely to give plausibility to one's slogan, and the opposition will suffer dislike and disrepute. Then once one takes a moral high ground by advocating and practicing the "right thing," political debates will be held over ethical superiority and inferiority – it is obviously the political binary code dressed in morality. We should also note that moralized politics can remove problems of feasibility and effectiveness of policies from the public's view.

For Noelle-Neumann (1984), Locke's consideration of "the law of opinion or reputation" provided a good angle to think about the fear of being isolated from the majority of fellow citizens. He discussed that nobody "can live in society under the constant dislike and ill opinion" (Locke, 2000, p. 257). However, social criteria of virtue and vice, esteem and discredit, do not promise a consensus. We can easily find a person who is esteemed by some but not esteemed by others. Locke also pointed out that moral judgment is rooted in our sense of good and bad, which is closely tied with our sense of "pleasure and pain," "love and hatred" (Locke, 2000, p. 163). Moral communication has a risk of becoming intolerant of different attitudes because those basic feelings can bring assertiveness to us. Today, people's opinions and reputations are expressed and circulating on the Internet. It is as if the once incapacitated "judging public" (Benjamin, 1999, p. 433) has woken up and found a new home in social media. Moral communication is constantly irritating society. This does not necessarily cause trouble that goes beyond a private dispute. However, a real problem arises when a gap in moral attitudes leads to a conflict at the collective level. Luhmann (2012, p. 244) writes, "morality takes on 'polemogenous', war-generating traits: it arises from conflicts and encourages conflicts." This will become more likely when political opportunism exploits an inflammable gap in society to gain political momentum.

3.3   Conflict and Society 1: Terrorism

The improbability of acceptance is one of the basic conditions of communication. It is quite usual to say "no" to others. We decline a proposal, refuse a request, and express a different opinion in our daily lives. Usually, the consequences of saying "no" are neutralized into civilized forms. However, sometimes they can be catalytic for forming an autonomous communication system. Luhmann (1995) defined *conflict* as a communicative process formed and organized through contradiction. Reaching an agreement or consensus can close a process of non-conflictive communication, such as negotiation and discussion. Conflict has a more stubborn nature of self-organization. Every society has a variety of seeds for disputes. Political partisanship, differences in moral attitudes, economic interests, ethnic identities, and religious faith can be reasons for conflicts. Conflicts with such reasons will inevitably become collective and can be destructive to the existing social order if politically agitated and exploited.

In conflict, one party's interest contradicts that of another party. In this zero-sum situation, one party's action pursuing its interest harms another party's. Therefore, stepping into a conflict can be very risky for each party.

However, if a party thinks it can persuade a third party of its justice or legitimacy, the risk of conflict would be calculated as acceptable. Morality and law offer a warranty for such optimistic risk assessment. "Morality, above all law, also works to promote conflict by clearly indicating that one's position lies on the side of right and by subjecting the opposing side to public rejection or even legal sanction" (Luhmann, 1995, p. 302). Conflict depends on rules and norms that make it possible to suppose what is right or not right in the court of law and public opinion.

It should be interesting if we remember that Luhmann's theory of the mass media and the empirical study of journalism observed "conflict" as one of the criteria of news selection (Luhmann, 2000a; Harcup & O'Neill, 2016). Those colliding with each other should know that they might be thrown into the spotlight of public attention by the news media. Once they catch the media's attention, they will prepare to pursue their causes and interests in front of the public's eye. In a lawsuit, conflicting parties may have press conferences and be willing to get interviewed by reporters. *Social movement* is another type of conflict in modern society (Luhmann, 1995, p. 398). Especially in a *protest movement*, a group of people say "no" to some parts of society, such as the government and companies. Sometimes "no" seems to target almost the entire society when a movement is tackling a global issue. Movements well-organized in terms of scale and style have a good chance of receiving public attention through the media and advocating their causes effectively. Traditionally, civic movements have been taking styles of physical demonstrations such as having a rally and marching on the street. Physical demonstrations at the heart of big cities, from the Great March on Washington in 1963 to Occupy Wall Street in 2011, were intensively reported and have become historical events. Recently, there are also online activities such as hashtag movements on social media like the #MeToo movement.

The limited scope of policymakers and mainstream media often creates the need for advocacy through social movements. "That society hitherto disregarded the topic or paid too little attention to it is the condition for the movement to develop." (Luhmann, 2013, p. 162) Jeffrey M. Berry (1999, p. 45) reported that between 1963 and 1991, the agendas of the U.S. Congress shifted from the "material issues," which are the traditional political issues like social security, taxation, and crime, to the "postmaterial issues," such as environment, human rights, and discrimination.[28] His finding shows that the political system has updated its sensitivity to social issues. However, that is not enough to

---

28   For the distinction of the "material" and the "postmaterial," see also Berry and Schildkraut (1998, p. 140).

cover the various issues in contemporary society. The same problem can be found in the case of journalism. Journalists cannot report every single topic in society. Social movements advocate issues and ideas which have not received the attention they deserve from policymakers and the public. Looking at the big picture, the political system, journalism, and social movements work as societal sensors for socially relevant issues.

In a society under the rule of law, violence is not accepted as a means of forcing others to accept one's own view. However, we have been witnessing illegal aggression in many parts of the world. We are familiar with calling some *terrorism* or a terrorist attack. Like the definition of populism, defining this other case of "-ism" phenomena has been controversial and elusive for scholars (Laqueur, 2001, p. 79; Laqueur & Wall, 2018, p. 31). Walter Laqueur (1996, p. 24), summarizing definitions of terrorism, wrote it is "the substate application of violence or threatened violence intended to sow panic in a society, to weaken or even overthrow the incumbents, and bring about political change." Here I focus on two points implicated in this working definition. First, terrorism intends to give a *shock* to society. Fritz B. Simon (2002, p. 14) describes terror as an act of causing a sudden and unexpected event that makes people feel they are under threat. The event must not be regarded as an ordinary accident or crime included in the list of typical troubles in society. A communication system forms its *structure as a complex of expectations in communication* (Luhmann, 1995). For instance, moral standards distinguish what is right or wrong in human behavior. Articles of criminal law are prepared for various crimes and provide sanctions for each offense. A physical assault case, especially a murder case, often becomes a news headline, but it does not cause a shock to the entire society. Terrorism goes beyond the threshold of the normal by its *extremism*, which is our second point. The extremism of terrorism appears in terms of its intensity of aggression and political objective. An explosion in crowded downtown tells us that something *unusual* has happened. In 2001, the September 11 attack in New York gave an impression to the people who witnessed the collapse of the World Trade Center that it was almost unreal. As the working definition cited above points out, terrorism pursues extreme political objectives, such as overthrowing a government and even toppling an existing political regime.

After the September 11 attacks, scholars tried to describe the communicative process triggered by the terrorist attack from the perspective of social systems theory. Wolfgang L. Schneider (2007, p. 132) formulated the binary code of terrorism as "successful attack" and "failed attack." Even if a physical attack is prevented by police, a plot of the attack itself – to be exact, information about the attack's threat – may have serious social and political consequences.

In 2006, the terror plot to detonate explosive devices on a flight from the U.K. failed, but the warning related to the plot caused a nationwide disruption for airlines. Schneider (2007, p. 134) argues that the failed attack should not simply be regarded as "failed." Societal response to a "terrorist" attack (or plot) depends on factors and conditions like its political significance, the readiness of the public security system, the amount of media attention, and the news media's perception of the attack.[29] From our perspective, responses at the communicative level are crucial to understanding how society deals with a crisis. "One of communication's most important achievements is sensitizing the system to chance, disturbances, and 'noise' of all kinds. In communication, one can make understandable what is unexpected, unwelcome, and disappointing" (Luhmann, 1995, p. 172). Today, the public's communicative response to the "unexpected" on the Internet undoubtedly constitutes part of the societal response. In 2015, after the deadly attacks in Paris, citizens shared the hashtag #JeSuisEnTerrasse on social media and expressed that they would not change their usual way of life. This movement was reported by traditional news media and supported on social media. In this case, the attacks were not prevented, but the outcome should not be what the perpetrators had intended. "Ironically, when a terrorist campaign has had an effect, it has more often than not been the opposite from the one desired" (Laqueur, 1999, p. 47). Those with a plot will face the unpredictability of societal response because society does not respond like a trivial machine. They may be able to ignore the outcomes and simply intend to cause devastation, but this will be an absolute denial to the world and become almost meaningless in the end.[30]

Scholars have pointed out that terrorism emerges in asymmetrical conflicts.[31] Politically motivated terrorism has to have a receiver of its message to start negotiation in order to attain its political goal. However, there are huge disparities in terms of military, economic, and technological power and status in the existing regime between terrorists and their opponents, in many cases, states (Stepanova, 2008). In normal circumstances, those who embrace an extremist ideology cannot be at the negotiating table with the government. Peter Fuchs (2004, p. 18) discussed that terrorism is a strategy to disrupt the conventional communicative process and initiate a different manner of

---

29   A comparative study on the usage of the "terrorist/terrorism" label in the coverage of Islamist and right-wing attacks between Western and non-Western media groups showed that both media applied the label more frequently to Islamist attacks (Chan et al., 2023).

30   Herfried Münkler (2001, p. 15) noted that there were cases of religious terrorism without any claims of responsibility, demands, or justification.

31   For the asymmetry of global political constellations in the early twenty-first century as the background of international terrorism, see also Münkler (2005).

communication through violence. Still, a terrorist's message must be received and understood to establish contact with its receivers (Fuchs, 2004, p. 20). This does not mean the message will be favorably understood and cause intended societal reactions. Given the significant disparities, terrorists have to obtain popular support in their social heartland. However, it is not an ordinary business because they have to persuade people that their violence, which costs human lives, is right and necessary.

Therefore, terrorism uses a more aggressive definition of its political opponent: "enemy" in Carl Schmitt's meaning (Schneider, 2007, p. 143). For Schmitt, "the political" is far more intense confrontation than usual political struggles in institutionalized party politics. It is the most extreme antagonism, which includes the possibility of armed conflict and negation of enemy's existence (Schmitt, 2007, pp. 29–33). Using this aggressive label of the opponent, terrorists intend to present that they are fighting a war for the cause of the people. This campaign must also be carried out through the media. In 2005, Ayman al-Zawahiri, a senior al-Qa'ida leader, wrote in his letter to a leader of the al-Qa'ida's Iraq branch that "we are in a battle, and that more than half of this battle is taking place in the battlefield of the media" (Federation of American Scientists, 2005). However, the media campaign does not promise to win the hearts and minds of the social heartland. From the systems theoretical point of view, the distinction between "friend" and "enemy" needs a *program* to allocate the positive and negative values to its subjects plausibly. Like other non-*political* conflicts, such as legal and private disputes, terrorism finds its occasion in existing interests, identities, and sentiments in society. In the case of international terrorism, which was intensively discussed after the September 11 attacks, a religious distinction such as "the Muslim" and "the heretics" was mobilized to make up a narrative of uncompromisable conflict (Kepel & Milelli, 2008, p. 264). It is important to note that neither religion nor other social conditions per se trigger a deadly conflict. We should rather take a close look at the modus operandi of escalation.

3.4 Conflict and Society II: Armed Conflict

During the armed conflict in Rwanda in the first half of the 1990s, the country's history was redefined as an enduring conflict between the Hutus and the Tutsis by a group of ideologues, which includes experts of history and philosophy from the Rwandan university (Kapuściński, 2001, p. 179). In the case of the armed conflict in Bosnia and Herzegovina, organized violence was used to sow "fear and hate" in society (Kaldor, 2012). In these cases, traditional mass media such as radio and television were the key media platforms to disseminate materials for escalation. A decade after those devastating conflicts, the spread of social media drastically changed the media and communication scape. We know that extremists like the Islamic State have been sowing fear and recruiting combatants through social media. At different intensity levels of conflict – from usual political struggles to armed conflict – views and information (including misinformation and disinformation) have been disseminated on the Internet. Various types of conflict constantly irritate society by communicating "no" to opponents' interests, thoughts, ways of life, and identities.

Luhmann (1995) pointed out that conflict tends to become "parasitic" in society and even absorb every kind of resource from its host society. We find an example of this phenomenon in the intolerance of neutral and moderate people. During the armed conflict in Bosnia and Herzegovina, those who were moderate and refused to hate other ethnic groups became the target of extreme nationalists (Kaldor, 2012, p. 58). Simon's (2004) typology of conflict helps us understand the nature of severe conflicts (Figure 10). The solid line shows that in a "strong conflict" one has to choose one's stance from two mutually excluded positions. If one supports one side, it logically means one is against the other. If one does not choose one's side, one becomes an opponent or enemy to both sides. Those engaging in a "strong conflict" get frustrated with the existence of neutral and moderate people who refuse to be involved in the conflict. The intolerance in a "strong conflict" forces people, including journalists, to support either side of the conflicting parties.

In his critical application of Luhmann's conflict theory to armed conflict, Krzysztof C. Matuszek (2007) formulated a conflict that is powerful enough to construct its entire structures as an "autopoietic" system of conflict. Once a conflict becomes "autopoietic," it mobilizes everything to organize itself and changes human behavior in many dimensions. In this situation, willingly or unwillingly, people start to behave as if they are already involved in the conflict, which can lead to further escalation. Aggressive exchanges such as "hateful attitudes, newspaper polemics, frictions between private persons and, ... mutually moralistic suspicions" tell people that society is now totally thrown into conflict. Through the process of escalation, according to Simmel (2009, pp. 295–296), "antagonism develops directly from all kinds of material

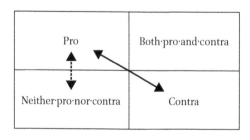

FIGURE 10
Strong and weak conflict
SIMON (2004:28)

relationships inside of peace." The "parasitic" conflict is destructive to the societal peace and civilized complexity of the host society. The drive of conflict is no longer restrained by societal rules such as laws, ethical codes, and traditional norms. The "autopoietic" conflict reinterprets meanings on hand and even revises history to organize its narrative. In this spiral of escalation, truth, the "first casualty" of war, becomes another name of politically desirable perception. News coverage – to rephrase Clausewitz – becomes the continuation of conflict. Legal standards and fundamental values like the Geneva Conventions and human rights can be misused to demonize enemies.

In contrast to a "strong" conflict, in a "weak conflict," shown by the broken line (Figure 6), people can keep their distance from the either/or choice. In this type of conflict, only those who have decided to support a particular side get involved in the conflict. One is not forced to make an either/or choice between conflicting parties. Normally, in a society where "strong" conflict is well deterred, this "weak" type of conflict prevails. Most people can continue to conduct second-order observation of conflict from a third party's point of view. So, as far as conflict stays "weak" and takes institutionalized forms, a variety of conflicts show us a landscape of contradictory interests, ideologies, and values in the host society. In this regard, we could say that conflict indicates societal dynamics.

In weak conflict, news media can maintain their autonomy as second-order observers. It means that media outlets' selectivity comes into play in reporting conflict. Conflict is part of the news values, but the choice of which conflicts to cover depends on their decisions. On the other hand, in some cases, the press serves as a medium to convey narratives of conflicting parties. "Through journalists, the parties in a conflict tell their stories, and their narratives change as the conflict develops" (Hamelink, 2011, p. 34). Journalistic autonomy becomes at risk, especially when reporters rely on powerful news sources, such as government announcements and briefings. To avoid this, journalists seek expert comments and hear voices of victims and displaced people. Today, people whose lives are threatened by armed conflicts can also publish their own narratives on social media (Patrikarakos, 2017). Narratives of conflicting parties simplify a situation into a confrontation between "enemy" and "friend" and involve us in this frame of perception. Narratives that see armed conflicts from those affected people tell us to distance ourselves from this view.

After World War I, Paul Valéry (1989, p. 30) wrote that peace is more complex than war. He meant that life is more complex than death and that conflict is part of our lives. However, it must be conducted in other ways than violence which brings about death. Luhmann (1995, p. 395) discussed that prohibiting the use of physical force makes conflict more complex, refined, and perpetuating. In a modern state with a monopoly on the legitimate use of physical force (Weber, 2008), one has to avoid using violence to conduct and resolve conflict. This restriction forces us to pursue our interests in ways the law permits. It will take time before finding a solution or compromise. But they will be pursued in a civilized manner compatible with societal diversity and stability. Here, by "stability," I do not mean that society will never change. Instead, it means that society, absorbing the impact of conflict, can change without falling apart. In this regard, conflict could be a catalyst for reformation, which makes society more sustainable in the long run.[32]

Part 4: News as Societal Observation

4.1   *Structural Change of the Media Constellation and Journalism*
Everything I have discussed in this book, such as governing, journalism, politics, and conflict, could not be studied without considering the impact of the contemporary communication environment. The list of media functioning and interrelating in society has become longer and longer. In other words, the societal "media system" (DeFleur & Ball-Rokeach, 1989, p. 304) is now more complicated than ever.[33] One of the most interesting outcomes of this development is that varieties of media have become closely connected to each other. In the late 1990s, Ronald Deibert (1997, pp. 114–115) observed that media were linked into "a single seamless web of digital-electronic-telecommunications." He argued that the communication environment of his time had dramatically changed by a complex of new media technologies, which he called "hypermedia." After the advent of social media, Andrew Chadwick (2017, pp. 4–5) introduced the term "hybrid media system," which focuses on the hybridization of "newer" and "older" media logics (technologies, genres, norms, behaviors, organizational forms) that conditions political communication. He underlines that various media, not only "newer" but also "older" ones, are coevolving and forming the contemporary communication environment of politics. In order to describe the reciprocal relations between the mass media and the web,

---

32   See also Luhmann (1995, pp. 371–372).
33   Denis McQuail (1992, p. 96) distinguished three levels of media performance research: macro (entire or national media system), meso (a particular sector of media industry such as national daily newspaper), micro (a particular news outlet such as a single newspaper title or television station). This book is most interested in the macro level of media performance. However, the other levels should also be interesting when we examine the autonomy or independence of journalism through a case study of particular sectors and news outlets.

Boccia Artieri and Gemini (2019) introduced a distinction between system and environment. The systems theoretical, or "ecological" approach intends to observe the relationship of two autonomous systems in the contemporary media constellation and eschew using notions such as "hybrid" and "liquidity," which blur the boundaries of these systems.

Through the 1980s and 1990s, media outlets became increasingly dependent on materials such as photos and video footage taken by ordinary citizens and freelancers. Considering the diversification of information-gatherers, Tara Sonenshine (1997) argued that the power of gatekeepers in news production had waned.[34] She wrote, "the 1980s and '90s have brought us new, sophisticated and high-tech tools – better camera lenses, hand-held video cameras, satellite dishes, and the Internet with its open invitation for the public to play reporter" (Sonenshine, 1997, p. 11). Actually, the Internet has made everyone who has access to it potential authors and reporters. Every day we see bloggers, including experts from various fields, posting numerous articles and tweets.

How can we describe the current status of news circulation? Axel Bruns (2003, 2005, 2018) discusses that a new role is emerging in today's communication environment. It is no longer called a "gatekeeper" but a "gatewatcher." Gatewatching is to keep an eye on news sources and tell people where relevant information is available. Gatewatchers are not only careful observers of information sources but also authors who produce their texts based on the available information. Gatewatchers do not control the gates through which information flows. Instead, they are curators of open-source information. Seth C. Lewis and Nikki Usher (2013, p. 612) think that journalists' role is such "curators" of information, and their task is "helping to bring together all of the accumulated knowledge that people have contributed across open-source platforms and social media venues." However, as Bruns (2018, pp. 355–356) notes, other actors with suitable expertise and experience can also take the curating role together with journalists.

Meanwhile, the gatekeeping model has been updated considering the audience's role and the changing situation of news channels. Lewin's original gatekeeping model sees two tracks in food distribution: gardening and buying

---

34   We may consider the decline of journalists' initiative in selecting news materials from another point of view: *tabloidization*. "*Tabloidization of content* is usually framed as trivialization, with celebrity gossip and human-interest stories crowding out serious news. Tabloidization is primarily audience- and advertiser-driven, in an increasingly competitive news environment" (Bird, 2015, p. 604, emphasis in the original). The newly recognized news value "shareability" proposed by Harcup and O'Neill (2016) should be interesting when we examine whether journalists' editing policy has become more audience-driven.

(Lewin, 1947). In this model, for instance, vegetables travel from a garden or grocery shop to our family table, and these two channels are separated from each other. Pamela J. Shoemaker and Tim P. Vos (2009) discuss that we will find more than two tracks if we apply Lewin's model to news circulation. More importantly, they also point out that news channels are not separated but interpenetrating. "Thus the channels are not fixed or impenetrable, but instead are fluid, and information flows between them on its way to the audience" (Shoemaker & Vos, 2009, p. 122). Then, we have to take multiple actors and channels into consideration in order to map the current news circulation.

4.2   "Source Cycle" between the News Media and the Blogosphere

Today, everyone with access to the Internet can have a personal website in various styles. This means that not only professional journalists but also other experts and ordinary citizens can disseminate their opinions and information. In the galaxy of websites, we observe that journalists and other participants are actively talking about topics from journalistic and non-journalistic sources. Here, I call the place of online communication through blogs and social media the *blogosphere*.[35] Stephen D. Cooper (2006, p. 129) discusses that the blogosphere, as well as mainstream media, decides topics on which people comment and how much attention is to be paid to those topics. He suggests that the blogosphere is fulfilling gatekeeping and agenda-setting functions, which have been attributed only to professional journalists. Shoemaker and Reese (2014, pp. 179–180) are interested in the fact that there are no longer walls between news channels. Every day, people talk about news topics reported by journalists. But on the other hand, photos and video footage posted on social media often appear in professional news reports.

Web portals providing information from diverse news outlets and individual authors are also popular places to access news. For instance, *Yahoo! News* is the most popular news site in Japan, Taiwan, and the United States (Newman et al., 2022). On *Yahoo! Japan*, for example, people find domestic news articles from supposedly conservative to liberal sources. The portal also provides hard and soft news from foreign news outlets such as BBC, CNN, and South Korean newspapers. Based on his survey of *Yahoo! Japan*'s users, Tetsuro Kobayashi (2013) reported that conservative users tended to think that newspapers and television stations had political biases. Regarding online news sites, the same

---

35   Rebecca Blood (2002) distinguished three types of weblogs: personal journals on writers' daily lives, notebooks including focused comments on personal or the external world, and filter blogs containing selected links to the Web. For empirical studies on the different types of blogs, see, for example, Herring et al. (2005) and Wei (2009).

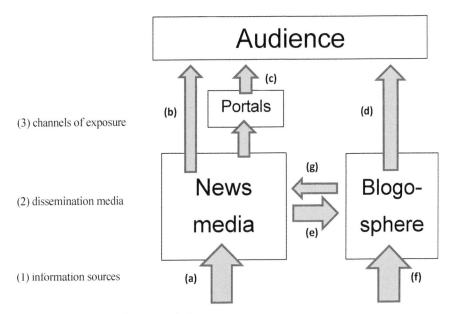

FIGURE 11   Structure of news circulation

perception was not observed. He suggested that the diversity of news sources on *Yahoo! News* should be associated with the result.[36]

Figure 11 is a diagram of the structure of news circulation discussed above. Traditional news media run by professional journalists are as powerful and trusted news sources as before. However, people's perception of media credibility changes yearly (a). Traditional communication technologies such as the printing press and broadcasting media are still critical for the news media. These days, websites have become familiar tools to provide news coverage to audiences (b). News articles are also circulating via popular web portals (c) and as newsfeeds through social media (d). Today, we observe the interchange of materials between the news media and the blogosphere. A significant percentage of news topics are provided to the blogosphere by the news media (e). The blogosphere is a vast platform where countless photos, video footage, and eyewitness stories are posted by those who happened to witness newsworthy events. We also find experts' analyses on various issues (f). For the

---

36   About 90% of his respondents who use online news sites named *Yahoo! News* as their favorite online news channel (Kobayashi, 2013, p. 127). According to the latest report (Newman et al., 2022), 56% use *Yahoo! News* at least once a week in Japan (only 11% use the second popular site, *Nippon TV news online*), whereas 40% in Taiwan (38% use the second popular site, *ETtoday online*) and 16% in the United States use it weekly (14% for *CNN.com*, the second popular site).

news media, the blogosphere is a virtual place to observe public opinion and a valuable field for gathering news materials (g).

Scholars in media and communication studies have been discussing the interrelationship between traditional news media and the blogosphere under the title of *intermedia agenda-setting*. Early research on intermedia agenda-setting focused on the influence between news media such as newspapers, television stations, and wire services.[37] Studies in the United States revealed that wire services and major news organizations such as the *New York Times* influenced the agendas of other news organizations (Du, 2017, p. 781). Based on their study of intermedia agenda-setting between traditional media (*New York Times* and *Washington Post*) and the blogosphere, Marcus Messner and Marica W. DiStaso (2008) reported that both were dependent on each other's materials and topics – especially on politics – and the interdependency emerged in the first half of the 2000s. Cooper (2006, p. 129) pointed out that the blogosphere became an alternative and supplementary news source for mainstream news media. As the blogosphere became recognized as an alternative source, journalists started to pay more attention to blogs. The growing media attention has increased the chance that blog posts will receive public attention. An agenda circulating back and forth between the traditional media and the blogosphere can increase its salience to the people and newsworthiness to journalists. This can propel the further transference of the agenda in society. Messner and DiStaso (2008) called this process a "source cycle."

Regarding the power balance in the source cycle, some scholars discussed that traditional media dominated agenda-setting in the blogosphere. Reese and colleagues (2007) found that top American news-related blogs relied heavily on news stories by professional journalism, and at the same time, the blogs promoted public dialogue about information and opinions reported by journalists. Mark Leccese (2009) demonstrated that almost half of the information sources linked by top political blogs in the United States were mainstream media. Other important sources like primary sources on the Web (for instance, websites of the government, think tanks, non-profit organizations, and political parties) were linked less than mainstream media. Kwak Haewoon and colleagues revealed that *Twitter* was rather a source of topics and information than a tool for social networking for most of its users. They also claimed, "Twitter users tend to talk about topics from headline news and respond to fresh news" (Kwak et al., 2010, p. 597). Based on their study of trending topics on *Twitter*, Sitaram Asur and colleagues (2011, p. 437) found that *Twitter* was

---

37   As for early examples of studies in the twentieth century, see Messner and DiStaso (2008, p. 448); Du (2017, pp. 780–782).

"a filter and an amplifier for interesting news from traditional media" such as CNN, the *New York Times*, and *ESPN*.

Brendan R. Watson (2012) put forward a different view. He demonstrated that bloggers interested in local public affairs like historic preservation were more likely to use original sources than traditional news media such as newspapers and television stations. In addition to geographical relevance, his finding also suggests that bloggers' dependency on traditional news sources varies according to interested categories of subjects. For example, Watson notes that mainstream media tend to cover subjects related to government more frequently than local history and the environment. This bias seems to limit bloggers' dependency on mainstream media in some fields. Henry Farrell and Daniel W. Drezner (2008) revealed that journalists paid more attention to blogs than the general population and suggested this explains why blogs sometimes have real political consequences despite their relatively low number of readers. The amplified influence of blogs is one of the most interesting outcomes of the source cycle between journalism and the blogosphere. Sharon Meraz (2011) showed that political blogs, regardless of their positions in the political spectrum (left-leaning, right-leaning, and moderate), influenced the setting of traditional media's online news agendas.[38] However, Kevin Wallsten (2007) observed "a complex, bidirectional relationship" between mainstream media coverage and blog discussion. The power balance between both sources should shift as the communication environment changes.

The perspective of intermedia agenda-setting studies had been based on the distinctions between traditional media and the Internet, or journalists and non-journalists. However, as many journalists participated in the blogosphere, the distinction between journalists and bloggers has blurred (Gunter et al., 2009). As mentioned, scholars pointed out the interdependence between traditional news media and the blogosphere (Messner & DiStaso, 2008; Meraz, 2011). We can no longer see the process of news production and circulation as simply as before (Du, 2017, p. 787). Frequent exchanges of information, images, and footage between multiple media platforms exist. Besides, news outlets have both traditional and online channels to distribute their content. The entire platform of news circulation has become a more "seamless web" of media.

---

38   For influences of the blogosphere on mainstream media coverage, see also Bogard and Sheinheit (2013). Messner and Bruce Garrison (2011) found that traditional news media (e.g., *CNN*, *New York Times*, *Washington Post*) cited political filter blogs more often as opinion sources than as factual ones.

Interestingly, the agenda-setting theory has started to pay more attention to the complex nature of agenda-setting today. Lei Guo and McCombs (2011) focused on the agenda-setting effect on *cognitive maps* of public agendas. This approach examines the "network agenda setting" model, which hypothesizes that the news media transfer salience of relationship between elements of an agenda, such as a political candidate's attributes. This model presumes that the news media can provide more integrated information than the traditional agenda-setting theory thought. The "network agenda setting" approach conceptualizes a schema as a sub-network in an individual's cognitive network (Guo, 2013, p. 114; Guo & McCombs, 2016, p. 10). The concept of schema has indicated that human cognition unifies elements of an object to organize its overall impression. At the most abstract level, a schema is a configured representation of attributes of an object (Fiske & Taylor, 2013). The agenda-setting approach pays attention to the fact that attributes included in a schema have some *salience* and, in this respect, a schema is a configuration of salient attributes (Guo & McCombs, 2016, p. 9).

Schema is also a relevant concept for the framing approach to news reporting. A news report is supposed to activate cognitive schemas of recipients, for instance, those related to an armed conflict. The reporter may stress its political background or a humanitarian crisis caused by the conflict. Either way, a group of cognitive schemas related to the topic will be activated. That is the cognitive framing of news reporting (Scheufele & Scheufele, 2010). However, this grouping effect inevitably entails selective activation. Robert M. Entman (1993) noted that framing has two key aspects of its function: *selection* and *salience*. "To frame is to *select some aspects of a perceived reality and make them more salient*" in communication (Entman, 1993, p. 52, emphasis in the original). However, in a complex society, framing by the news media may encounter different perspectives and counter-framing.

Scholars have examined framing effects on audiences. Shanto Iyengar (1987) found that stories focused on particular victims (rather than government policies and economic situations) tended to activate causal attribution of poverty to individual victims. Joseph N. Cappella and Kathleen H. Jamieson (1997) compared the effects of "strategic framing" and "issue framing." They found that the strategic framing, which makes politicians' conflict, self-interest, and political tactics salient, activated distrust in politics. Strategic framing drew the public's attention to the motives or intentions of political actors. Attributing motives and intentions to persons is a usual manner of observation in communicative processes. However, referring to intention may cause a sincerity problem (Luhmann, 1995, p. 150). Even the most unquestionable sincerity, expressed in condolences, can be questioned in a political context. Jamieson and Capella (2008, pp. 204–205) showed that listeners of the Rush Limbaugh Show were likely to think President Clinton's admiration for his cabinet member, who died in a plane accident in 1996, was uttered for his political advantage. It is no wonder that there are differences in interpretations of reported realities. However, strategic framing, whether by journalists or audiences, may cultivate a skeptical, not necessarily cynical, attitude toward people in the spotlight.

4.3   Communication and Surplus Meanings

Does the structural change in news circulation have implications for the societal construction of meaning? This section will go through a theoretical account to find our path to describe the condition of communication and news in contemporary society. Baecker (2006, 2007a, 2007b) discussed that the unprecedented "overflow of meaning" has been brought about by introducing the computer, which processes information as digital data and enhances the capacity to disseminate and store information. As seen before, Luhmann noted that writing and the printing press had drastically increased the comparability in communication. The comparability heightened by the computer implies that we face an unprecedented excess of available information.

New information has some implications for interpreting meanings. Subsequently, meanings will be reinterpreted in the extended range of referable information. In this regard, we never walk into the same flow of information twice. In a practical context, when we assess the effectiveness of a public policy, we continue to read updates on its implementation and consider the latest results. The past reports will become irrelevant or simply obsolete through this examination process. The enhanced flow and stock of information may disturb this process. However, when we play a game of chess, we do not have to know every past move. We only work in the present, where we deal with the accumulated results of past decisions (Watzlawick et al., 2011, p. 8; Luhmann, 2012, pp. 349–350). At the cognitive level, schemas and framing operate to give configurations of information in our hands.

However, processing meanings under the constant flow of information must be done in the societal turmoil due to the global pandemic, geopolitical tensions, and other current circumstances. Considering the societal experience of the COVID-19 pandemic, Habermas (2020) said we had learned that we, including experts, had so many things we could not know, estimate, and predict. The awareness of ignorance will lead to careful acceptance of information. However, the situation is complicated. The circulation of "problematic information" (Giglietto et al., 2019) such as false or misleading information, which is recently called "infodemic," has caused the problem of information reliability. It should be quite a challenge for contemporary society to absorb the impact of random mutation of meanings and construct common knowledge.

Luhmann's concept of "meaning" was intensively discussed first in the early 1970s. Luhmann (1971a) sees that every actual experience implicitly or explicitly refers to other possibilities in three dimensions: *factual, temporal,* and *social.* When we have a conversation, we have to choose a topic properly from potential topics, and the choice should be made at the right time if we want to have it smoothly. Each choice is attributed to a particular participant, but other participants may be interested in different topics. It is unavoidable that we make such a choice in communication. Luhmann stresses that given experience and action always refer to other possibilities. "The phenomenon of meaning appears as a surplus of references to other possibilities of experience and action" (Luhmann, 1995, p. 60). His concept of "meaning" describes the condition of processing meaning in a complex society where diverse values and perspectives are involved in communication. In his terminology, "complexity" (Luhmann, 1995, p. 25) means that our experience and action always appear as a result of choice, which can be reviewed later by ourselves or someone else. Interestingly, Luhmann's modal concept of "meaning" was articulated when the possibility of mass second-order observation expanded after the unprecedented growth of information consumption since the 1950s (Figure 1).

Luhmann (2012, p. 248) conjectured that we could find some modes of processing surplus meanings that characterize a particular state of society and help it deal with its surplus meanings. For instance, a *purpose* that Aristotle discussed as *telos* in ancient Greece, which experienced the impact of the alphabet and writing, offered a perspective to evaluate and organize available possibilities. *Telos* means that every human action is, by nature, directed toward a final state that is to be aimed (Brennan, 2005). The idea of *nature* worked as a foundation to determine what would or should happen. The heightened comparability brought about by the printing press forced constant reviewing of interpretations. One has to be ready to take account of different or updated information and examine whether past interpretations are still defensible. Communicating in the modern condition implies constant self-examination and the capability to learn from new information and others' points of view.

Baecker (2007a, 2011) argues that we are living in a "next" state of surplus meanings. The circumstances demand a new concept to describe communication under the condition of amplified surplus possibilities. Communication has been formulated as a mode of interaction between information processing units such as sender/receiver (Shannon & Weaver, 1963), ego/alter (Parsons, 2012; Luhmann, 1995), and non-trivial machines (von Foerster, 2003). For

Baecker (2005, pp. 19–20), information helps us to infer what the world is like. When a bookstore clerk tells us the location of the book we are looking for, we will also think that other related books are on the shelves nearby. Baecker focuses more sharply on communication's information processing function. He reformulated communication as an operation toward finding orientation in the world of uncertainty through information processing (Baecker, 2005, p. 22).

Baecker's reformulation of communication is articulated by introducing Spencer-Brown's (2021) concept of "form" that operationalizes our conduct of knowing. It says that we always make a distinction when we refer to something. Distinction creates both "marked" and "unmarked" states. Spencer-Brown defined the entire space of "marked" and "unmarked" states as a "form" of the distinction. Anything "marked" could be replaced with other possibilities latent in "unmarked" space. For instance, the letter "A" handwritten on a whiteboard indicates other alphabetical letters such as "B," "C," and so forth. If we want, we can erase "A" and write another letter instead. The concept tells us that there are latent possibilities every time we refer to something and that actualizing latent possibilities needs another operation. A second-order observation may reveal both sides, namely a "form" of a distinction. For Baecker (2005, pp. 75–76), communication is a mode of operation to handle "forms" of distinctions and find orientation despite surplus possibilities. Communication can refer to anything. However, every reference indicates other possibilities that would occasionally be mentioned later on in communication. Baecker notes that communication is thus combining first- and second-order observations.

Schutz and Luckmann (1974, pp. 163–167) discussed the "intransparency" of the life-world, that is, the fundamental provisionality of human knowledge and its elements. They state, "the relative opacity of the life-world is read off not only from the 'positive' aspects of the stock of knowledge, the credibly determined elements of knowledge, but also from the 'negative' determinations contained in the horizon of these elements of knowledge" (Schutz & Luckmann, 1974, p. 167). We acquire knowledge from our experience and learning opportunities. However, thus acquired knowledge remains fundamentally provisional and open to revision in the future. As seen in the shift from the Ptolemaic view to the Copernican one, even once self-evident knowledge can lose its credibility and be revised. Priorities and time constraints inevitably make us selective in acquiring knowledge and can interrupt sufficient explication of knowledge. A negated element of knowledge is not simply deleted but overlaid by a new element and would be reevaluated occasionally. A change of situation and long-term observation also move us to update our knowledge.

In the late 1990s, Kraut and his colleagues revealed that the data did not support an assumed effect of the Internet as a social technology of communication ("Internet paradox"). Their follow-up research found that Internet use was associated with increasing social relationships.

In order to deal with surplus possibilities, communication installs a mechanism that reduces uncertainty. From chatting to a formal conversation, it involves expectations about participants' behavior. Expectations of proper or usual behavior in a given situation work as structures of the communicative process because they bring rules and assumptions to the practice. However, we also observe that unexpected conduct goes against our expectations. Here, we can find another example of "form" that works in communication (Baecker, 2005, pp. 88–89). The "form" of expectation deals with certainty and uncertainty in communication. We know that the unexpected may happen anytime. Therefore, politeness sometimes gives us a heartwarming surprise, and we feel satisfied when we do not have to trigger a contingency plan. Expectation provides communication with the capability to detect and handle something disturbing. In this respect, based on its expectational structure, communication finds a chance to build its "order from noise." However, if we take Baecker's argument seriously, we should raise the following questions. Given the heightened level of surplus possibilities, how can society create its "semantics" and common knowledge? How can we describe the implications of the circumstances for news reception in society?

4.4   *News as Self-Descriptions of Society*

Several terms and phrases have been coined to describe contemporary society, such as "information society" and "globalized society." Luhmann noted that these expressions are "imaginary constructions" (Luhmann, 2013, p. 167) that enable us to talk about society as a whole. From his systems theoretical point of view, those communicative descriptions of society are *self-descriptions* of society. Fuchs (1992, p. 88) discussed "unification semantics (Einheitssemantik)," which constructs a unity of society despite the functionally differentiated structure of society.[39] Benedict Anderson (2006) demonstrated that nations are "imagined communities" that are products of societal construction in the modern society equipped with the printing press. For Luhmann (1990b; 2012), society is an encompassing system of communication. He thinks that conceptualizing society as an entity belongs to the Western tradition of thought. A description

---

39   Klaus P. Japp (2003) applied this concept to Islamic fundamentalism.

of "imaginary" unity may give us a landscape or picture of society, but at any rate, it must be distinguished from the actual flow of communication.[40]

The term *self*-description tells that society becomes reflexive to itself. Then what does reflexivity do in describing society? When we describe society using a distinction such as "eco-friendly" and "not eco-friendly." We refer not only to "eco-friendly" products and companies but also to "not eco-friendly" ones. In this case, seeing both sides of the distinction is not difficult. When news articles use such words as "democracies" and "the West," we know that the marked contents connote something relevant but opposite to them. We should see "autocracies" and "authoritarian regimes" on the other side of "democracies." "The West" has a more complex arrangement that includes "the East" in two different meanings (the Communist countries and countries of Asia) and other non-Western categories. The examples of societal descriptions show that each category works as a "form" that cleaves the world into two spaces. Baecker (2005, p. 139) sees that society's self-description describes "forms" working in societal observations. However, unlike sociological descriptions, it does not intend to reflect upon distinctions applied to its subject. The following passage of an article in the *Financial Times* uses the above-mentioned distinctions to indicate the existing differences between regimes and countries. "An *authoritarian* wave that began outside the established *democracies* of *the west* has spread to the US and Europe. The resurgence of *authoritarian* attitudes and practices that first manifested itself in young *democracies*, such as Russia, Thailand and the Philippines, has spread into *western* politics" (Rachman, 2017, emphasis added). In this regard, the self-description of society is not interested in finding alternative distinctions to describe society. Instead, it repeatedly uses existing distinctions and conventionalizes them.

For Baecker (2005, pp. 141–142), *news* is a distinctive form of self-description of society. A government announcement of a successful result of its policy implementation offers us an opportunity to observe an unmentioned negative side of it. Reporters are likely to mention unwelcome outcomes of the policy implementation. By referring to both mentioned and unmentioned sides, an article can reveal a "form" of the distinction unspokenly made by the announcement. Like other societal descriptions, news reports can also be subjects of second-order observations. Readers can talk about their unmentioned

---

40 Simmel (2007) saw drawing a landscape as cutting out a piece of nature and forming a unity from its infinite interconnection of things. For Susan Sontag (2007, pp. 124–125), photography is a modern way of seeing which reduces the unlimited complexity of the real. "To see reality in the light of unifying ideas has the undeniable advantage of giving shape and form to our experience. But it also – so the modern way of seeing instructs us – denies the infinite variety and complexity of the real."

sides. From the perspective of second-order observers, news reporting cleaves the world into *reported* and *not-reported* sides. Therefore, the reported topics and potential news materials constitute a "form" of news reporting.[41] The existence of the other side does not immediately mean that news reporting becomes useless in society. Rather, as Luhmann (2012, p. 14) writes, communication "itself generates and tests the ignorance necessary for its continued operation." People sometimes complain about the newsroom's selectivity or "biases," but they still talk about reported topics and their follow-ups. In this respect, the ignorance of news reporting facilitates public communication and makes opinions visible in the public sphere.

To sum up, news as a self-description of society constructs recognizable realities, which we can mention in daily conversation, assuming people have already shared them. It also reveals distinctions drawn in societal descriptions. However, compared to sociology and art, journalism focuses on providing conventional descriptions of society. Journalism is a reflecting and reproducing factor in the societal construction of meaning. The increased comparability of knowledge and the general accessibility to the Internet have changed the condition of news reception. Second-order observations of not-reported sides put the selectivity of news coverage in the public eye. Having selectivity is fine because every field has priorities. The question lies in the societal role of their selective information handling.

Part 5: Observing News and Media in a Complex Society

5.1   *Journalism as Investigative Curator*

Max Weber's interest in newspaper study, expressed in the early twentieth century, offered sociologists a starting point to discuss the condition of beliefs and knowledge in the era of the mass media. Weber (2016, p. 268) mentioned a British press baron, Lord Northcliffe,[42] and raised a question about the outcomes of trustification in the newspaper industry. The press baron reportedly said, "God made people read so that I could fill their brains with facts, facts, facts – and later tell them whom to love, whom to hate, and what to think" (Cudlipp, 1980, p. 82). He thought that he could dominate "facts" and agendas in society. However, today we cannot be so naive about the power of news outlets. As seen before, intermedia agenda-setting studies have discussed the

---

41   Baecker (2005, p. 142) formulates this as *mass media's* "form."
42   He is also known as the director of the *Enemy Propaganda Department*, or "Crewe House," during World War I (Stuart, 2013, p. 8; Taylor, 1999, p. 6).

"source cycle" between traditional news media and the blogosphere. Some scholars observed that mainstream media still have the dominant power over agenda-setting in the blogosphere. Other scholars pointed out that journalists are paying attention to the blogosphere, which sometimes has real political consequences that are newsworthy for news outlets.

The development of information sources on the Internet has prompted scholars to redefine the societal role of journalism. Unlike the traditional role of "gatekeepers," "gatewatchers" are not expected to control the information supply to the public. Instead, they are careful observers of open information sources and authors of socially relevant articles published on traditional news media and the Internet. Scholars have also started to use the word "curators" to describe journalists' role in society. News "curators" are supposed to have a good eye for reliable sources and information with societal *relevance* or *actuality*. Diversified social problems have increased the need for expertise in various fields, such as environmental science, gender studies, education, and public health. The diversified need for reliable information and knowledge will develop the specialization of news "curators."

The traditional understanding of journalism assigns the "watchdog" role to journalists. As far as the public supports this idea, news reporters will continue to be in charge of societal self-description of public matters. They will continue to investigate what is happening and reveal unobserved sides of society. They will also raise the alarm and tell there is a problem that requires the public's urgent attention. However, here we have to raise a question already suggested in the systems theory of journalism. Is journalism the only player to conduct such second-order observation? The answer to this question should be negative. Experts on various issues, such as university scientists and think tank analysts, can research in their fields and examine policy implementation. Citizens who do not have particular expertise can take part in a critical examination of public policy, especially when it has to do with their community. Recently, a contemporary investigative journalism style specializing in open-source intelligence (OSINT) has shown its effectiveness and grown its presence in the public sphere. Considering the whole circumstances, we may say that journalism is the societal investigative curator who sorts out newsworthy events, collects information from reliable sources, investigates undisclosed facts, and publishes reports on socially relevant matters.

5.2 *Reporting for Governing?*

Since the late twentieth century, the newspaper industry and journalism have experienced economic and identity crises. Some American journalists led movements for reshaping the profession, called *public journalism* or *civic journalism*, which intended to find a new way to report socially relevant issues and engage in society. *The Charter Declaration for Public Journalism* says they "believe the diversity and fragmentation of society call for new techniques for storytelling and information-sharing to help individual communities define themselves singularly and as part of the whole set of communities" (Charter Members of the Public Journalism Network, 2003). In the 1990s, scholars had started to discuss the phenomena such as polarization, culture war, fragmentation, and cyberbalkanization in the United States (e.g., Hunter, 1991; DiMaggio et al., 1996; Van Alstyne & Brynjolfsson, 1996).[43] Jay Rosen (1999, p. 262), one of the leading advocates of the movement, stressed the importance of seeing people as potential actors, encouraging communities to deal with public affairs, and making "the climate of public discussion" more constructive. We find cases of this community-based approach to redefining the societal role of journalism in local American newspapers such as *The Wichita Eagle* and *The Charlotte Observer*.[44] However, the movement stirred up a controversy in the profession, especially over journalism's independence, objectivity, and duty. Leonard Downie, *Washington Post* executive editor, said, "Too much of what's called public journalism appears to be what our promotion department does." In the eyes of the traditional mindset, strengthening cooperation with citizens was risky for journalism. For Richard Aregood, *Philadelphia Daily News* editorial page editor, asking about what journalists should do for communities is "abandoning a piece of our own jobs" (Case, 1994, p. 14).

In 2003, the *Pew Center for Civic Journalism* closed its history as "the most important institutional vehicle for the public journalism movement" (Haas, 2007, p. 19). This episode tells us that the movement lost its momentum in the early 2000s (Madison & DeJarnette, 2018, p. 17). In the decade after the institution's close, we saw the rapid spread of social media and the expansion of the blogosphere. Seeing the development of open-source information platforms, Lewis and Usher (2013, p. 612) wrote that journalists "would be curators in a community conversation." What does this statement mean after all the movement of "making journalism more public"[45] and the controversy over the duty of journalism?

---

43   These trends have been broadly discussed. Recent studies deal with, for example, the effects of access to partisan media outlets (e.g., Lelkes et al., 2017) and link recommendation algorithms (e.g., Santos et al., 2021), the relationship between cyberbalkanization and mass polarization (e.g., Chan & Fu, 2017; Lee et al., 2019).

44   For community-oriented journalism studies and practices, see also Reader and Hatcher (2012) and Wenzel (2020).

45   The paper title of Jay Rosen (1991).

First, the statement suggests that rethinking journalism's societal role continues. We find interesting movements of constructive, or solution-oriented journalism. *The Solutions Journalism Network*, founded in 2013 in the United States, thinks that not only problems but also responses to them are newsworthy. Solutions journalism focuses on processes of tackling problems that have often dropped from the traditional scope of news coverage. For this movement, it is an essential part of journalism to report responding efforts in communities and, importantly, their limitations of effectivity and applicability to other communities (Solutions Journalism Network, n.d.). The *Constructive Institute*, established in 2017 in Denmark, advocates the importance of *constructive journalism*. Ulrik Haagerup (2017, pp. 15–17), the organization's founder, agrees that journalism is facing the fundamental challenge of finding its societal role in the contemporary communication environment. He raises a question about why the news media have been unequally thinking of a "negative" or "bad" story as a "good" news story. He admits that reporting outbreaks of a deadly virus, terror attacks, and the war continues to be necessary. However, to rethink the role of journalism, he argues that the constructive side of society (like people's extraordinary efforts to make things better) should be newsworthy.[46]

We can say that the advocates share the vision of journalism as a more "socially embedded activity" and are making efforts to cultivate practical "learning communities" (Scott, 2021, p. 83) by reconsidering the societal role of journalism. Put in this book's terms, these movements are advocating the idea that journalism is an essential part of *governing*, or collective efforts to find solutions to shared problems. However, skepticism and disagreement expressed by journalists show that the debate in the profession is not likely to end any time soon (Haagerup, 2017, pp. 88–90). The energetic debates also show that the profession has a strong motivation for its autonomy by distinguishing between *journalistic* and *non-journalistic* practices. We could say that the autonomy of journalism can change its shape or at least add a new element to its practice that does not conflict with the profession's duty. If "telling the truth" about our social and political reality is one of the primary tasks of journalism, reporting should cover both the problematic and the constructive sides of society (Haagerup, 2017, p. 91).

The role concept "curator" suggests where to find another implication for journalism. The rapid growth of user-generated information on the Internet has eroded news outlets' monopoly on investigating and disseminating socially

---

46   See Hopkinson and Dahmen (2021) for scholarly examinations of solutions and constructive journalism.

relevant information. Journalists are still prominent investigators and distributors of such information. However, today scholars are discussing that they are also navigators in the sea of information, searching for reliable sources and putting information together to describe current affairs. Can we still call such reports "news"? We could say "yes." However, it depends on whether the public will continue to regard news as the product of journalism. Experienced journalists Paul Brighton and Dennis Foy (2007, p. 194) write that they have been tackling a persistent question, "Why is this news?" and their answer may remain, "It just is!" This answer implies that news is news because it is presented as "news" by journalists or news outlets. Is Marcel Duchamp's Fountain an artwork because it was submitted by an artist? Duchamp's presentation in 1917 famously provoked a fundamental question: "What is art?" The semantics of "news" may survive the era of digital media and the massive flow of information.

However, we have various styles of societal descriptions such as think tank analysis, social scientific papers, and assessment reports of civic groups, government, and international organizations. Journalistic observation has to find its advantage over other styles of societal observation. Luhmann (2000a) sees the function of the mass media in generating familiar objects and their daily updating. Creating familiarity needs general understandability for a broad audience. As its etymological root shows, the daily updating of information is a core element of journalism. Working in the midst of the rapid flow of information is part of the job. It is hard to keep up with the tempo of journalistic practice for scientific research and other technical work unless they are highly routinized and standardized, like meteorological updates. Considering these aspects, we can say that the semantics of "news" will be under continuous reconsideration compared with other styles of societal description against the backdrop of the transforming public sphere. Possibly "news" would continue to be regarded as journalistic reports. It is also likely that it will mean a broader range of reports on current issues in society. If so, "news" will be provided in increasingly diversified styles and contexts than before. Various would-be news providers, who have their own social, political, and commercial purposes, will play their parts on the public stage. However, in any case, their contribution to governing matters most to the practical minds in struggling communities.

5.3   Media as Societal Facilitators for Problem-Solving

Norbert Elias stated that meaning is created not by an isolated individual (*Homo clausus*) but by people who communicate in social life. "What we call 'meaning' is constituted by people in groups who are dependent on each other in this or that way and can communicate with each other" (Elias, 2001, p. 54).

In the 1950s, prominent studies of mass society and totalitarianism pointed out that isolation from society, especially intermediary groups where people work together for common purposes, is the chief characteristic of the human condition in mass society (Arendt, 1969, p. 317; Kornhauser, 1960, p. 41). After seeing the early stage of the Internet era, Robert D. Putnam (2000, p. 177) warned that "individualized entertainment and commerce rather than community engagement" would be emphasized by the commercially-led development of the Internet. Having an abundant variety of communication tools and opportunities, we are still not sure whether we are not alone (Turkle, 2011). Today, political agitation and extremism use various social networking tools to disseminate messages and reach people in precarious conditions. As Proverbs (6:12) said, wicked plots are still going around with crooked speech in the twenty-first century. We know that many young people were lured to Syria by the Islamic State, and so-called troll factories are engaging in battles of information and narratives on the Internet (Singer & Brooking, 2018; Patrikarakos, 2017; Pomerantsev, 2019).

In the current conditions, a variety of communities and associations may offer social places for mitigating isolation and participating in the social construction of meaning. Solution-oriented communities and associations can be common frameworks that motivate collective efforts to tackle public problems such as environmental protection, preservation of cultural heritage, disaster management, and various human rights issues. We may think such efforts will likely build or revitalize local communities. The spatial dimension of communities has a multi-layered structure from neighborhood to global levels. News media and the blogosphere can play important roles in sharing information and supporting actors dealing with societal challenges. A concept of "societal media" was proposed to articulate the media's mediating function in governing efforts. When the media support and encourage actors by (1) sharing public issues and goals, (2) helping actors' resource procurement such as fundraising and recruiting, or (3) facilitating their collaboration, they work as societal facilitators for solutions (Takahashi, 2015b, 2019) (Figure 12).[47] Traditional news media update and disseminate socially relevant information. They, intentionally or not, prepare common knowledge to understand the significance of actors' contributions. The movements of solutions journalism and constructive journalism are motivated to engage more directly in social solutions. Social media and blogs offer open online forums for public agenda-setting and social networking. All forms of media appears as "societal media" when

---

47   This figure first appeared in Takahashi (2019, p. 604). I slightly modified it for use in this book.

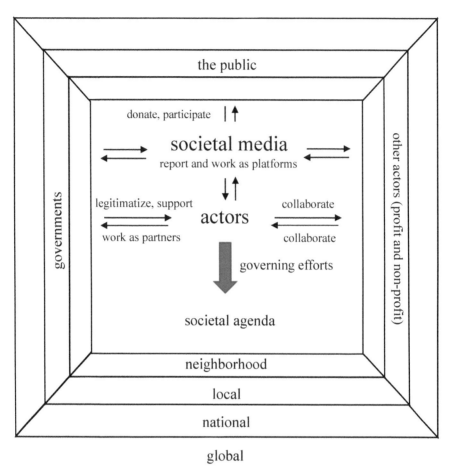

FIGURE 12   Societal media as facilitators of governing efforts

they contribute to practical efforts for problem-solving. This concept intends to bring more attention to the potential of the constructive use of media in a complex society.

If solution-oriented communities and associations successfully use the media's potential, they can contribute to building societal *resilience*, that is, society's capability to handle collective problems. "Resilience" is a key term in disaster response and management. UNDRR (*United Nations Office for Disaster Risk Reduction*) defines resilience to disasters as "the ability of a system, community or society exposed to hazards to resist, absorb, accommodate, adapt to, transform and recover from the effects of a hazard in a timely and efficient manner" (UNDRR, 2017). This social ability is important for not only disaster management but also other kinds of problem-solving. Societal resilience can be demonstrated in every corner of society by people's improvised actions. Most of them are ephemeral, but this is how society appears.

Seen from a long-term perspective, modernization and globalization in the last several centuries have been causing severe impacts on communities all over the world. Conflicts in the international community have been causing turbulence in trade, scientific research, and cultural exchanges. The disturbing factors will not be removed in the foreseeable future. There are no handy and quick solutions to the circumstances. In the legacy of sociology, we find an insight that tells us a way to construct our common meaning. "Collective representations are the product of a vast cooperative effort that extends not only through space but over time; their creation has involved a multitude of different minds associating, mingling, combining their ideas and feelings – the accumulation of generations of experience and knowledge" (Durkheim, 2001, p. 18). The media constellation has drastically changed in the last decades. However, the fundamental condition of meaning construction stays unchanged. Our only choice is to use media technology wisely and reinvent the media as societal media. Our practical unisolated mind is a compass for navigating the sea of information filled with siren voices.

Summary and Conclusions

This book treated news reporting as a changing stream of the social construction of meaning. Since the 1990s, traditional news media's monopoly on the dissemination of information has been undermined, and the space of communication on public subjects (the "public sphere") has expanded. The scholars have formulated the autonomy of the journalism system in the public sphere, regarding journalism as a provider of socially relevant information in the functionally differentiated society.

Since the 2000s, when the major social media platforms launched, intermedia agenda-setting researchers have focused on the interdependence of the news media and the blogosphere. The growth of user-created content in the blogosphere has also impacted our understanding of the social role of journalism. Journalists have become "curators" who collect and provide socially relevant and reliable information to their audiences rather than "gatekeepers" who control the societal source of information. Some community-oriented practitioners emphasized the importance of journalism's constructive role, that is, its contribution to problem-solving processes in communities. It is still contentious in the profession but offers a reflective perspective from which to consider "journalism in society."

Many vortexes swirling in society seek to involve as many people as possible through strategic dissemination of information. Politics and conflict are powerful examples. They intervene in the public sphere and its news reception. A structural interdependence between the news media and politics can be observed. Politics is the source of news content for the news media, and politics learns voters' perceptions from reported realities. In this interdependence, morality plays a key role on both sides. The news media refer to moral codes when reporting politicians' misbehavior, and politicians do the same when taking the moral high ground against their rivals. Interestingly, the scholars have found moral dichotomies (e.g., "the pure people" versus "the corrupt elite") at the core of populist messages. There is no doubt that morality constitutes the normative structure of society. However, from a practical point of view, we may question whether or how moral politics can solve our concrete problems on the ground.

The most radical forms of conflict, such as terrorism and armed conflict, justify the use of violence and involve people through their messaging tricks. The friend/enemy distinction that defines a deadly enemy constructs a "strong conflict" that does not tolerate neutrality. In many cases, terrorists are under an "asymmetrical" balance of power with powerful opponents such as states. To compensate for this inferiority, terrorists must win popular support in their political or religious heartlands. However, the effectiveness of the terrorist messages is increasingly uncertain in the global online public sphere. The systems theorists have explored the autonomy of terrorism and armed conflict as communication processes and defined them as "parasites" on society. They discuss that terrorist attacks depend on the structure of social expectations to bring about a strong impression of unexpectedness, or a shock to society. Armed conflict, which mobilizes everything from human lives to cultural identities, becomes profoundly destructive to its host society.

The modus operandi of political confrontation and conflict escalation must be under careful observation. Information curation by journalists in the public sphere should include addressing inflammatory messages. As the *Institute for Propaganda Analysis* shows, activities against propaganda by civic groups (including professionals) are also important. In recent years, OSINT groups such as *Bellingcat* have attracted attention in fact-checking and investigative journalism. Unorganized and improvised responses on social media (such as adding notes to problematic posts) can contribute to cultivating societal resilience against false, deceptive, or misleading information.

News has long been understood as daily updates on socially relevant events and issues provided by professional journalists. The semantics of "news" may further enrich the traditional understanding if journalists continue to be the most powerful information provider to the public by investigating and curating socially relevant information. However, there are a variety of sources giving such updates today. So, "news" can become a more generic word for updates on society among various forms of updates from non-journalistic sources. Tracing the semantic change of this word should be a pivotal point for examining whether journalism maintains its distinctive role in contemporary society.

For Sociocybernetics, communication, information, and meaning are fundamental subjects. The meaning construction is a multilayered phenomenon involving physical, mental, and social processes. Felix Geyer treated meaninglessness as paralyzed information processing at the individual level. The problem of information overload can also be observed at the communicative level. The meaning construction through the dissemination and reception of news occurs in the very short term. The rapid cycle of news consumption may obscure the information processing problem in society. However, second-order observers can compare reported topics with other socially relevant issues in terms of newsworthiness. In this respect, reporting reproduces the distinction between what is reported and what is not reported. Journalists will continue to be second-order observers of politicians and conflicting parties and tell the truth inconvenient to them. Observing and being observed, journalism engages in forming eigenvalues through selective reporting and second-order observation.

The work in this book needs to be complemented by further studies with different approaches and focus. A series of analyses based on an operationalized conception of information and meaning is oriented toward measuring communications (e.g., Leydesdorff & Ivanova, 2014; Leydesdorff et al., 2017; Leydesdorff et al., 2018; Leydesdorff, 2021). This approach extends Shannon's mathematical theory of communication in order to handle meaning and tries to show how cultural evolution is shaped. Historical studies of the sociology of knowledge on ideas and realities disseminated through the media and prevailed at a particular time would consider historical changes in social structures and communication environments (e.g., Luhmann, 1986). Research on intercultural conversation in local society points to the importance of researchers' participation in the conversation process as social and cultural changes happen in inhabitants' interactional and psychic spaces (Sidorova et al., 2020). As sociologists, we somehow participate in what we are observing. In this regard, what we are explaining is what we are experiencing (Maturana & Verden-Zöller, 2008). I think that the fundamental conditions of inter-human communication have not changed. Nevertheless, it is an interesting task to carefully examine what recent algorithmic developments have changed in human-machine interaction (e.g., Esposito, 2022). Of particular interest is how the selectivity in the construction of meaning changes when algorithms are used on a large scale.

References

Albertazzi, D., and McDonnell D. eds. (2008). *Twenty-First Century Populism: The Spectre of Western European Democracy*. New York: Palgrave Macmillan.

Anderson, B. (2006). *Imagined Communities: Reflections on the origin and spread of nationalism (Revised edition)*. London; New York, N.Y.: Verso.

Arendt, H. (1969). *Origins of Totalitarianism*. Cleveland: World Publishing.

Arlen, M.J. (1982). *Living-Room War*. New York: Penguin.

Artificial Intelligence Art and Aesthetics Research Group, ed. (2019). *Artificial Intelligence Art and Aesthetics Exhibition*. Artificial Intelligence Art and Aesthetics Research Group.

Ashby, W.R. (1968). Variety, Constraint, and the Law of Requisite Variety. In: W. Buckley, ed., *Modern Systems Research for the Behavioral Scientist*. Chicago: Aldine, pp. 129–136.

Asur, S., Huberman, B.A., Szabo, G., and Wang, C. (2011). Trends in Social Media: Persistence and Decay. In: *Proceedings of the International AAAI Conference on Web and Social Media* 5(1), pp. 434–437. https://doi.org/10.1609/icwsm.v5i1.14167.

Baecker, D. (1996). Oszilierende Öffentlichkeit. In: R. Maresch, Hrsg., *Medien und Öffentlichkeit: Positionierungen, Symptome, Simulationsbrüche*. Berlin: Boer, pp. 89–107.

Baecker, D. (2005). *Form und Formen der Kommunikation*. Frankfurt am Main: Suhrkamp.

Baecker, D. (2006). Niklas Luhmann in the Society of the Computer. *Cybernetics and Human Knowing* 13(2), pp. 25–40.

Baecker, D. (2007a). Communication with Computers, or How Next Society Calls for an Understanding of Temporal Form. *Soziale Systeme* 13(1/2), pp. 407–418.

Baecker, D. (2007b). The Network Synthesis of Social Action I: Towards a Sociological Theory of Next Society. *Cybernetics and Human Knowing* 14(4), pp. 9–42.

Baecker, D. (2011). What is Holding Societies Together? On Culture Forms, World Models, and Concepts of Time. *Criticism* 53(1), pp. 1–22.

Bas, O., and Grabe, M.E. (2015). Sound Bite. In: G. Mazzoleni, ed., *The International Encyclopedia of Political Communication*. https://doi.org/10.1002/9781118541555.wbiepc063.

Bateson, G. (2000). *Steps to an Ecology of Mind: Collected Essays in Anthropology, Psychiatry, Evolution, and Epistemology*. Chicago: University of Chicago Press.

Baudrillard, J. (1994). *Simulacra and Simulation*. Ann Arbor: University of Michigan Press.

Bauman, Z. (2000). *Liquid Modernity*. Cambridge: Polity Press.

Beck, U., Giddens, A., and Lash, S. (1994). *Reflexive Modernization: Politics, Tradition and Aesthetics in the Modern Social Order*. Cambridge: Polity Press.

Benjamin, W. (1999). *Selected Writings Volume 2 1927–1934*. Cambridge, Mass.: Belknap Press of Harvard University Press.

Benjamin, W. (2008). *The Work of Art in the Age of Mechanical Reproduction*. London: Penguin.

Berger, P.L. (1967). *The Sacred Canopy: Elements of a Sociological Theory of Religion*. Garden City, N.Y.: Doubleday.

Berger, P.L., and Luckmann, T. (1980). *The Social Construction of Reality: A treatise in the sociology of knowledge*. New York: Irvington Publishers.

Bernays, E.L. (1928). *Propaganda*. New York: Horace Liveright.

Bernays, E.L. (1961). *Crystallizing Public Opinion*. New York: Horace Liveright.

Berry, J.M. (1999). *The New Liberalism: The Rising Power of Citizen Groups*. Washington, D.C.: Brookings Institution Press.

Berry, J.M., and Schildkraut, D. (1998). Citizen Groups, Political Parties, and Electoral Coalitions. In: A.N. Costain and A.S. McFarland, eds., *Social Movements and American Political Institutions*. Lanham: Rowman & Littlefield, pp. 136–156.

Bird, S.E. (2015). Tabloidization. In: W. Donsbach, ed., *The Concise Encyclopedia of Communication*. Chichester: Wiley Blackwell.

Blöbaum, B. (1994). *Journalismus als soziales System: Geschichte, Ausdifferenzierung und Verselbständigung*. Opladen: Westdeutscher Verlag.

Blood, R. (2002). *The Weblog Handbook: Practical advice on creating and maintaining your blog*. Cambridge, MA: Perseus Publishing.

Boccia Artieri, G., and Gemini, L. (2019). Mass Media and the Web in the Light of Luhmann's Media System. *Current Sociology Monograph* 67(4), pp. 563–578.

Bogard, C.J., and Sheinheit, I. (2013). Good Ol' Boy Talk versus the Blogosphere in the Case of Former Senator George Allen. *Mass Communication and Society* 16, pp. 347–368.

Boydstun, A.E. (2013). *Making the News: Politics, the media, and agenda setting*. Chicago: University of Chicago Press.

Brennan, T. (2005). Telos. In: *The Shorter Routledge Encyclopedia of Philosophy* [eBook edition]. Routledge, p. 1014.

Brier, S. (2008). *Cybersemiotics: Why information is not enough!* Toronto: University of Toronto Press.

Brighton, P., and Foy, D. (2007). *News Values*. London: Sage.

Brownlees, N. (2006). Polemic Propaganda in Civil War News Discourse. In: N. Brownlees, ed., *News Discourse in Early Modern Britain: Selected Papers of CHINED 2004*. Berlin: Peter Lang.

Bruns, A. (2003). Gatewatching, Not Gatekeeping: Collaborative Online News. *Media International Australia* 107, pp. 31–44.

Bruns, A. (2005). *Gatewatching: Collaborative Online News Production*. New York: Peter Lang.

Bruns, A. (2018). *Gatewatching and News Curation: Journalism, social media, and the public sphere*. New York: Peter Lang.

Buchinger, E. (2007). Applying Luhmann to conceptualize public governance of auto-poietic organizations. *Cybernetics and Human Knowing* 4(2–3), pp. 173–187.

Camus, A. (1975). *The Myth of Sisyphus*. Harmondsworth: Penguin.

Canovan, M. (2005). *The People*. Cambridge: Polity Press.

Cappella, J.N., and Jamieson, K.H. (1997). *Spiral of Cynicism: The Press and the Public Good*. New York; Tokyo: Oxford University Press.

Case, T. (1994). Public Journalism Denounced. *Editor & Publisher* 127(46), pp. 14–15.

Chadwick, A. (2017). *The Hybrid Media System: Politics and Power*. 2nd ed. Oxford: Oxford University Press.

Chan, C-h., and Fu, K-w. (2017). The Relationship Between Cyberbalkanization and Opinion Polarization: Time-series analysis on Facebook pages and opinion polls during the Hong Kong Occupy Movement and the associated debate on political reform. *Journal of Computer-Mediated Communication* 22, pp. 266–283. https://doi.org/10.1111/jcc4.12192.

Chan, C-h., Wessler, H., Jungblut, M., Welbers, K., Althaus, S., Bajjalieh, J., and Van Atteveldt, W. (2023). Challenging the Global Cultural Conflict Narrative: An auto-mated content analysis on how perpetrator identity shapes worldwide news cover-age of Islamist and right-wing terror attacks. *International Journal of Press/Politics*, online first. https://doi.org/10.1177/19401612231157655.

Charter Members of the Public Journalism Network. (2003, January 25). *A Declaration for Public Journalism*. Public Journalism Network. http://pjnet.org/charter/.

Cohen, M.D., March, J.G., and Olsen, J.P. (1972). A Garbage Can Model of Organizational Choice. *Administrative Science Quarterly* 17(1), pp. 1–25.

Cooley, C.H. (1962). *Social Organization: A study of the larger mind*. New York: Schocken Books.

Cooper, S.D. (2006). *Watching the Watchdog: Bloggers as the Fifth Estate*. Spokane, Washington: Marquette Books.

Cottle, S. (2006). *Mediatized Conflict: Developments in media and conflict studies*. Maidenhead: Open University Press.

Creel, G. (2015). *How We Advertised America: The first telling of the amazing story of the Committee on Public Information that carried the gospel of Americanism to every corner of the globe*. [S.l.]: Scholar's Choice.

Cronin, T.E. (1980). *The State of the Presidency*. 2nd ed. Boston: Little, Brown and Company.

Cudlipp, H. (1980). *The Prerogative of the Harlot: Press barons & power*. London: Bodley Head.

D'Angelo, P. (2017). Framing: Media frames. In: P. Rössler, C.A. Hoffner, and L. van Zoonen, eds., *The International Encyclopedia of Media Effects, Volume II*. Chichester: Wiley Blackwell, pp. 634–644.

Davis, R. (2001). *The Press and American Politics: The new mediator.* 3rd ed. Upper Saddle River, N.J.: Prentice Hall.

DeFleur, M.L., and Ball-Rokeach, S.J. (1989). *Theories of Mass Communication.* 5th ed. New York: Longman.

Deibert, R. (1997). *Parchment, Printing, and Hypermedia: Communication and World Order Transformation.* New York: Columbia University Press.

Denton Jr., R.E. (1988). *The Primetime Presidency of Ronald Reagan: The era of the television presidency.* New York: Praeger.

Diamond, E., and Bates, S. (1992). *The Spot: The rise of political advertising on television.* 3rd ed. Cambridge, Mass.: MIT Press.

Diamond, E., McKay, M., and Silverman, R. (1993). Pop Goes Politics: New Media, Interactive Formats, and the 1992 Presidential Campaign. *The American Behavioral Scientist* 37(2), pp. 257–261.

DiMaggio, P., Evans, J., and Bryson, B. (1996). Have American's Social Attitudes Become More Polarized? *American Journal of Sociology* 102(3), pp. 690–755.

Dodds, G.G., and Rozell, M.J. (2000). The Press and the Presidency: Then and now. In: P.G. Henderson, ed., *The Presidency Then and Now.* Lanham, Md.: Rowman & Littlefield, pp. 139–160.

Du, Y.R. (2017). Intermedia Agenda-Setting Effects. In: P. Rössler, C.A. Hoffner, and L. van Zoonen, eds., *The International Encyclopedia of Media Effects, Volume II.* Chichester: Wiley Blackwell, pp. 779–791.

Durkheim, E. (2001). *The Elementary Forms of Religious Life.* Oxford: Oxford University Press.

Eco, U. (1995, June 22). *Ur-Fascism: Freedom and liberation are an unending task.* The New York Review of Book. June 22. https://www.nybooks.com/articles/1995/06/22/ur-fascism/.

Eco, U. (2006, October 8). *Umberto Eco: Attenti a internet troppe informazioni inattendibili.* La Repubblica. https://ricerca.repubblica.it/repubblica/archivio/repubblica/2006/10/08/umberto-eco-attenti-internet-troppe-informazioni-inattendibili.html.

Elias, N. (2001). *Loneliness of the Dying.* New York: Continuum.

Entman, R.M. (1993). Framing: Toward clarification of a fractured paradigm. *Journal of Communication* 43(4), pp. 51–58.

Esposito, E. (2002). *Soziales Vergessen: Formen und Medien des Gedächtnisses der Gesellschaft.* Frankfurt am Main: Suhrkamp.

Esposito, E. (2008). Social Forgetting: A systems-theory approach. In: A. Erll and A. Nünning, eds., *Cultural Memory Studies: An International and Interdisciplinary Handbook,* Berlin: De Gruyter, pp. 181–189.

Esposito, E. (2016). The Forms of Web-memory. In: G. Sebald, and J. Wagle, eds., *Theorizing Social Memories: Concepts and contexts,* London: Routledge, pp. 159–170.

Esposito, E. (2017). An Ecology of Differences: Communication, the Web, and the question of borders. In: E. Hörl and J. Burton, eds., *General Ecology: The New Ecological Paradigm*. London; New York: Bloomsbury, pp. 283–301.

Esposito, E. (2022). *Artificial Communication: How algorithms produce social intelligence*. Cambridge, Mass.: MIT Press.

Ess, C., ed. (1996). *Philosophical Perspectives on Computer-Mediated Communication*. New York: State University of New York Press.

Farrell, H., and Drezner, D.W. (2008). The Power and Politics of Blogs. *Public Choice* 134, pp. 15–30.

Federation of American Scientists (2005). *Letter from al-Zawahiri to al-Zarqawi*. Federation of American Scientists Intelligence Resource Program. http://www.fas .org/irp/news/2005/10/dni101105.html.

Feldman, O. (2004). *Talking Politics in Japan Today*. Brighton: Sussex Academic Press.

Fiske, S.T., and Taylor, S.E. (2013). *Social Cognition: From brains to culture*. Los Angeles: SAGE.

Friedland, L.A. (1996). Electronic Democracy and the New Citizenship. *Media, Culture & Society* 18, pp. 185–212.

Fuchs, P. (1992). *Die Erreichbarkeit der Gesellschaft: Zur Konstruktion und Imagination gesellschaftlicher Einheit*. Frankfurt am Main: Suhrkamp.

Fuchs, P. (2004). *Das System »Terror«: Versuch über eine kommunikative Eskalation der Moderne*. Bielefeld: transcript Verlag.

Galtung, J., and Ruge, M.H. (1965). The Structure of Foreign News. *Journal of Peace Research* 2, pp. 64–91.

Geyer, F. (1976). Individual Alienation and Information Processing: A systems theoretical conceptualization. In: F. Geyer, and D.R. Schweitzer, eds., *Theories of Alienation: Critical perspectives in philosophy and the social sciences*. Leiden: Nijhoff, pp. 189–223.

Geyer, F. (1980). *Alienation Theories: A general systems approach*. Oxford; New York: Pergamon Press.

Geyer, F. (1995). The Challenge of Sociocybernetics. *Kybernetes* 24(4), pp. 6–32.

Geyer, F., ed. (1996). *Alienation, Ethnicity, and Postmodernism*. Westport, Conn.; London: Greenwood Press.

Geyer, F., and Heinz, W.R., eds. (1992). *Alienation, Society, and the Individual: Continuity and change in theory and research*. New Brunswick, N.J: Transaction Publishers.

Geyer, F., and Schweitzer, D.R., eds. (1976). *Theories of Alienation: Critical perspectives in philosophy and the social sciences*. Leiden: Nijhoff.

Geyer, F., and Schweitzer, D.R., eds. (1981). *Alienation: Problem of meaning, theory and method*. London; Boston: Routledge & Kegan Paul.

Geyer, F., and van der Zouwen, J., eds. (1986). *Sociocybernetic Paradoxes: Observation, control and evolution of self-steering systems*. London: Sage.

Gibson, B. (2007). Sociocybernetics. In: M. Bevir, ed., *Encyclopedia of Governance, Volume 2*. Thousand Oaks, CA: Sage, pp. 897–901.

Giddens, A. (1991). *Modernity and Self-Identity: Self and society in the late modern age*. Cambridge: Polity Press.

Giglietto, F., Iannelli, L., Valeriani, A., and Ross, L. (2019). 'Fake News' is the Invention of a Liar: How false information circulates within the hybrid news system. *Current Sociology Monograph* 67(4), pp. 625–642.

Goffman, E. (1959). *The Presentation of Self in Everyday Life*. Garden City, N.Y.: Doubleday.

González, J., Amozurrutia, J.A., and Maass, M. (2016). *Cibercultur@ e iniciación en la investigación interdisciplinaria*. Ciudad de México: Universidad Nacional Autónoma de México (UNAM).

Görke, A. (1999). *Risikojournalismus und Risikogesellschaft: Sondierung und Theorieentwurf*. Opladen: Westdeutscher Verlag.

Görke, A. (2003). Das System der Massenmedien, öffentliche Meinung und Öffentlichkeit. In: K.-U. Hellmann, K. Fischer, and H. Bluhm, Hrsg., *Das System der Politik: Niklas Luhmanns politische Theorie*. Wiesbaden: Westdeutscher Verlag, pp. 121–135.

Görke, A., and Kohring, M. (1996). Unterschiede, die Unterschiede machen: Neuere Theorieentwürfe zu Publizistik, Massenmedien und Journalismus. *Publizistik* 41, pp. 15–31.

Graber, D.A. (1984). *Processing the News: How people tame the information tide*. New York: Longman.

Groys, B. (2018). *In the Flow*. London; New York: Verso.

Gunter, B., Campbell, V., Touri, M., and Gibson, R. (2009). Blogs, News and Credibility. In: *Aslib Proceedings*. 61(2), Emerald Publishing Limited, pp. 185–204. https://doi.org/10.1108/00012530910946929.

Guo, L. (2013). Toward the Third Level of Agenda-setting Theory. In: T. Johnson, ed., *Agenda Setting in a 2.0 World: A tribute to Maxwell McCombs*. New York: Routledge, pp. 112–133.

Guo, L., and McCombs, M. (2011, May). *Network Agenda Setting: A third level of media effects* [Conference presentation]. The International Communication Association Annual Conference, Boston, MA.

Guo, L., and McCombs, M., eds. (2016). *The Power of Information Networks: New directions for agenda setting*. New York: Routledge.

Haagerup, U. (2017). *Constructive News: How to save the media and democracy with journalism of tomorrow*. Aarhus: Aarhus University Press.

Haas, T. (2007). *The Pursuit of Public Journalism: Theory, practice, and criticism*. New York: Routledge.

Habermas, J. (1987). *Lifeworld and System: A critique of functionalist reason* (*The Theory of Communicative Action, Volume 2*). Boston: Beacon Press.

Habermas, J. (1998). Learning by Disaster? A diagnostic look back on the short 20th century. *Constellations* 5(3), pp. 307–320.

Habermas, J. (2020, April 15). *Jürgen Habermas über Corona: „So viel Wissen über unser Nichtwissen gab es noch nie."* Frankfurter Rundschau. https://www.fr.de/kultur /gesellschaft/juergen-habermas-coronavirus-krise-covid19-interview-13642491 .html.

Hahn, A. (1987). Sinn und Sinnlosigkeit. In: H. Haferkamp and M. Schmid, Hrsg., *Sinn, Kommunikation und soziale Differenzierung: Beiträge zu Luhmanns Theorie sozialer Systeme.* Frankfurt am Main: Suhrkamp, pp. 155–164.

Hallin, D.C. (1986). *The "Uncensored War": The media and Vietnam.* New York: Oxford University Press.

Hamelink, C.J. (2011). *Media and Conflict: Escalating evil.* Boulder: Paradigm Publishers.

Harcup, T., and O'Neill, D. (2001). What is News? Galtung and Ruge revisited. *Journalism Studies* 2(1), pp. 161–280.

Harcup, T., and O'Neill, D. (2016). What is News: Gaining and Ruge Revisited (again). *Journalism Studies* 18(12), pp. 1470–1488.

Harris, R. (1983). *Gotcha!: The media, the government, and the Falklands crisis.* London: Faber and Faber.

Harste, G. (2021). *The Habermas-Luhmann Debate.* New York: Columbia University Press.

Herring, S.C., Scheidt, L.A., Wright, E., and Bonus, S. (2005). Weblogs as a Bridging Genre. *Information Technology and People* 18(2), pp. 142–171.

Hofmannsthal, H von. (1991). *Sämtliche Werke, Band. 31.* Frankfurt am Main: S. Fischer.

Hopkinson, K.M., and Dahmen, N.S., eds. (2021). *Reporting Beyond the Problem: From civic journalism to solutions journalism.* New York: Peter Lang.

Hornung, B. (2019). The Challenges for Sociocybernetics. *Current Sociology Monograph* 67(4), pp. 511–526.

Hug, D.M. (1997). *Konflikte und Öffentlichkeit: Zur Rolle des Journalismus in Sozialen Konflikten.* Opladen: Westdeuscher Verlag.

Hunter, J.D. (1991). *Culture Wars: The struggle to define America.* New York: BasicBooks.

Institute for Propaganda Analysis. (1938). How to Detect Propaganda. *Bulletin of the American Association of University Professors* 24(1), pp. 49–55.

in't Veld, R.J., Schaap, L., Termeer, C.J.A.M., and van Twist, M.J.W., eds. (1991). *Autopoiesis and Configuration Theory: New approaches to societal steering.* Dordrecht: Kluwer.

Iyengar, S. (1987). Television News and Citizens' Explanations of National Affairs. *The American Political Science Review* 81(3), pp. 815–832.

Jagers, J., and Walgrave, S. (2007). Populism as Political Communication Style: An empirical study of political parties' discourse in Belgium. *European Journal of Political Research* 46(3), pp. 319–345.

Jameson, F. (1973). The Vanishing Mediator: Narrative Structure in Max Weber. *New German Critique* 1, pp. 52–89.

Jamieson, K.H., and Cappella, J.N. (2008). *Echo Chamber: Rush Limbaugh and the Conservative Media Establishment.* New York: Oxford University Press.

Japp, K.P. (2003). Zur Soziologie des fundamentalistischen Terrorismus. *Soziale Systeme* 9(1), pp. 54–87.

Kaldor, M. (2012). *New and Old Wars: Organised violence in a global era.* 3rd ed. Cambridge: Polity.

Kapuściński, R. (2001). *The Shadow of the Sun: My African life.* London: Penguin.

Kepel, G. and Milelli, J.-P., eds. (2008). *Al Qaeda in its Own Words.* Cambridge, Mass.: Belknap Press of Harvard University Press.

Kickert, W. (1993). Complexity, Governance and Dynamics: Conceptual exploration of public network management. In: J. Kooiman, ed., *Modern Governance: New government-society interactions.* London: Sage Publications, pp. 191–204.

Kobayashi, T. (2013).「マスメディアよりも『中立』な日本のネットニュース」[The online news platform in Japan is more "neutral" than traditional news media]. In: S. Kiyohara and K. Maeshima, eds.,『ネット選挙が変える政治と社会：日米韓に見る新たな「公共圏」の姿』[Politics and Society Changed by Elections on the Internet: The new "public sphere" in Japan, the U.S., and South Korea]. Tokyo: Keio University Press, pp. 119–147.

Kohring, M. (1997). Die Funktion des Wissenschaftsjournalismus: Ein systemtheoretischer Entwurf. Opladen: Westdeutscher Verlag.

Kohring, M. (2006). Öffentlichkeit als Funktionssystem der modernen Gesellschaft: Zur Motivationskraft von Mehrsystemzugehörigkeit. In: A. Ziemann, Hrsg., *Medien der Gesellschaft – Gesellschaft der Medien.* Konstanz: UVK, pp. 161–181.

Kohring, M. (2016). Journalismus als Leistungssystem der Öffentlichkeit. In: M. Löffelholz and L. Rothenberger, Hrsg., *Handbuch Journalismustheorien.* Wiesbaden: Springer, pp. 165–176.

Kohring, M., and Hug, D.M. (1997). Öffentlichkeit und Journalismus. Zur Notwendigkeit der Beobachtung gesellschaftlicher Interdependenz. *Medien Journal* 21(1), pp. 15–33.

Kooiman, J. (2003). *Governing as Governance,* London: Sage.

Kornhauser, W. (1960). *The Politics of Mass Society.* London: Routledge.

Kovach, B., and Rosenstiel, T. (2021). *The Elements of Journalism, Revised and Updated.* 4th ed. New York: Crown.

Kraut, R., Patterson, M., Lundmark, V., Kiesler, S., Mukopadhyay, T., and Scherlis, W. (1998). Internet Paradox: A Social Technology That Reduces Social Involvement and Psychological Well-Being? *American Psychologist* 53(9), pp. 1017–1031.

Kraut, R., Kiesler S., Boneva, B., Cummings J., Hegelson, V., and Crawford A. (2002). Internet Paradox Revisited. *Journal of Social Issues* 58(1), pp. 49–74.

Kwak, H., Lee, C., Park, H., and Moon, S. (2010). What is Twitter, a Social Network or a News Media? In: *Proceedings of the 19th International World Wide Web Conference*. ACM Digital Library, pp. 591–600. https://dl.acm.org/doi/10.1145/1772690.1772751.

Laclau, E. (1977). *Politics and Ideology in Marxist Theory: Capitalism, fascism, populism*. London: NLB.

Laity, M. (2015). NATO and the Power of Narrative. In: *Information at War: From China's three warfares to NATO's narratives*. London: Legatum Institute, pp. 22–28. Retrieved October 13, 2022, from https://li.com/reports/information-at-war-from-chinas-three-warfares-to-natos-narratives/.

Lakoff, G. (2016). *Moral Politics: How liberals and conservatives think*. Chicago: University of Chicago Press.

Lanzara, G.F. (1983). Ephemeral organizations in extreme environments: Emergence, strategy, extinction. *Journal of Management Studies* 20(1), pp. 71–95.

Laqueur, W. (1996). Postmodern Terrorism. *Foreign Affairs* 75(5), pp. 24–36.

Laqueur, W. (1999). *The New Terrorism: Fanaticism and the arms of mass destruction*. New York: Oxford University Press.

Laqueur, W. (2001). *A History of Terrorism*. New Brunswick, N.J.: Transaction Publishers.

Laqueur, W., and Wall, C. (2018). *The Future of Terrorism: ISIS, Al-Qaeda, and the Alt-Right*. New York, N.Y.: Thomas Dunne Books.

Lasswell, H. (2013). *Propaganda Technique in the World War*. Mansfield Centre, CT: Martino Publishing.

Laszlo, E. (1986). Systems and Societies: The basic cybernetics of social evolution, In: F. Geyer, and J. van der Zouwen, eds., *Sociocybernetic Paradoxes Observation, Control and Evolution of Self-steering Systems*. London: Sage, pp. 145–171.

Latour, B. (2005). *Reassembling the Social: An introduction to actor-network-theory*. Oxford: Oxford University Press.

Leccese, M. (2009). Online Information Sources of Political Blogs. *Journalism & Mass Communication Quarterly* 86(3), pp. 578–593.

Lee, F.L.F., Liang, H., and Tang, G.K.Y. (2019). Online Incivility, Cyberbalkanization, and the Dynamics of Opinion Polarization During and After a Mass Protest Event. *International Journal of Communication* 13, pp. 4940–4959.

Lelkes, Y., Sood, G., and Iyengar, S. (2017). The Hostile Audience: The effect of access to broadband Internet on partisan affect. *American Journal of Political Science* 61(1), pp. 5–20.

Leydesdorff, L. (1994). The Evolution of Communication Systems. *Systems Research and Information Science* 6, pp. 219–230.

Leydesdorff, L. (2010). The Communication of Meaning and the Structuration of Expectations: Giddens' "Structuration Theory" and Luhmann's "Self-Organization". *Journal of the American Society for Information Science and Technology* 61(10), pp. 2138–2150. https://doi.org/10.1002/asi.21381.

Leydesdorff, L. (2021). *The Evolutionary Dynamics of Discursive Knowledge*. Cham, Switzerland: Springer.

Leydesdorff, L., and Ivanova, I.A. (2014). Mutual redundancies in interhuman communication systems: Steps toward a calculus of processing meaning. *Journal of the Association for Information Science and Technology* 65(2), pp. 386–399. https://doi.org/10.1002/asi.22973.

Leydesdorff, L., Johnson, M., and Ivanova, I. (2018). Toward a Calculus of Redundancy: Signification, codification, and anticipation in cultural evolution. *Journal of the Association for Information Science and Technology* 69(10), pp. 1181–1192. https://doi.org/10.1002/asi.24052.

Leydesdorff, L., Petersen, A.M., and Ivanova, I. (2017). The Self-Organization of Meaning and the Reflexive Communication of Information. *Social Science Information* 56(1), pp. 4–27.

Lewin, K. (1943). Forces Behind Food Habits and Methods of Change. *Bulletin of the National Research Council* 108, pp. 35–65.

Lewin, K. (1947). Frontiers in Group Dynamics II. Channels of Group Life: Social planning and action research. *Human Relations* 1, pp. 143–153.

Lewis, S.C., and Usher, N. (2013). Open Source and Journalism: Toward new frameworks for imagining news innovation. *Media, Culture & Society* 35(5), pp. 602–619.

Lindell, M.K., Prater, C., and Perry, R.W. (2007). *Introduction to Emergency Management*. Hoboken, N.J.: Wiley.

Lippmann, W. (2018). *Public Opinion*. [s.l.]: Adansonia.

Little, J.H. (2001). Autopoiesis and Governance: Societal steering and control in democratic societies. In: F. Geyer and J. van der Zouwen, eds., *Sociocybernetics: Complexity, Autopoiesis, and Observation of Social Systems*. Westport, CT: Greenwood Press, pp. 159–170.

Locke, J. (2000). *An Essay Concerning Human Understanding*. Kitchener, Ontario: Batoche Books.

Luhmann, N. (1971a). Sinn als Grundbegriff der Soziologie. In: J. Habermas and N. Luhmann, *Theorie der Gesellschaft oder Sozialtechnologie: Was leistet die Systemforschung?* Frankfurt am Main: Suhrkamp, pp. 25–100.

Luhmann, N. (1971b). Öffentliche Meinung. In: N. Luhmann, *Politische Planung*, Opladen: Westdeutscher Verlag, pp. 9–34.

Luhmann, N. (1980). *Gesellschaftsstruktur und Semantik: Studien zur Wissenssoziologie der modernen Gesellschaft*, Frankfurt am Main: Suhrkamp.

Luhmann, N. (1986). *Love as Passion: The codification of intimacy*. Cambridge: Polity Press.

Luhmann, N. (1987). Autopoiesis als soziologischer Begriff. In: H. Haferkamp and M. Schmid, Hrsg., *Sinn, Kommunikation und soziale Differenzierung: Beiträge zu Luhmanns Theorie sozialer Systeme*, Frankfurt am Main: Suhrkamp, pp. 307–324.

Luhmann, N. (1990a). *Die Wissenschaft der Gesellschaft*. Frankfurt am Main: Suhrkamp.

Luhmann, N. (1990b). The World Society as a Social System. In: N. Luhmann, *Essays on Self-reference*, New York: Columbia University Press.

Luhmann, N. (1991). Wie lassen sich latente Strukturen beobachten? In: P. Watzlawick and P. Krieg, Hrsg., *Das Auge des Betrachters: Beiträge zum Konstruktivismus. Festschrift für Heinz von Foerster*. München; Zürich: Piper, pp. 61–74.

Luhmann, N. (1992). Die Beobachtung der Beobachter im politischen System: Zur Theorie der Öffentlichen Meinung. In: J. Wilke, Hrsg., *Öffentliche Meinung: Theorie, Methoden, Befunde, zu Ehren von Elisabeth Noelle-Neumann*. Freiburg: K.Alber, pp. 77–86.

Luhmann, N. (1993). Antwort auf Heinz von Foerster. *Teoria Sociologica* 2, pp. 85–88.

Luhmann, N. (1994). "What is the Case?" and "What Lies Behind It?": The Two Sociologies and the Theory of Society. *Sociological Theory* 12(2), pp. 126–139.

Luhmann, N. (1995). *Social Systems*, Stanford: Stanford University Press.

Luhmann, N. (1997). Limit of Steering. *Theory, Culture & Society* 14(1), pp. 41–57.

Luhmann, N. (2000a). *The Reality of Mass Media*. Stanford: Stanford University Press.

Luhmann, N. (2000b). *Die Politik der Gesellschaft*. Frankfurt am Main: Suhrkamp.

Luhmann, N. (2004). *Law as a Social System*. Oxford: Oxford University Press.

Luhmann, N. (2012). *Theory of Society, Volume 1*. Stanford: Stanford University Press.

Luhmann, N. (2013). *Theory of Society, Volume 2*. Stanford: Stanford University Press.

Maass, M. (2018). Proposal for the Development of a Thinking Culture as a Large System Formed by Multiple Sub-systems. In: M. Lisboa and D. Cerejo, eds., *Complexity Sciences: Theoretical and Empirical Approaches to Social Action*. Newcastle upon Tyne: Cambridge Scholars Publishing, pp. 46–63.

Machiavelli, N. (2005). *The Prince*. Oxford: Oxford University Press.

Madison, E., and DeJarnette, B. (2018). *Reimagining Journalism in a Post-Truth World: How late-night comedians, Internet trolls, and savvy reporters are transforming news*. Santa Barbara, Calif.: Praeger.

Mancilla, R. (2020). *Sociocybernetics and Political Theory in a Complex World: Recasting Constitutionalism*. Leiden; Boston: Brill.

Mandelbaum, M. (1982). Vietnam: The Television War. *Daedalus* 111(4), pp. 157–169.

Manning, M. (2004). *Historical Dictionary of American Propaganda*. Westport, Conn.: Greenwood Press.

Marcuello-Servós, C. (2018). Introduction: Sociocybernetics framework. In: M. Lisboa and D. Cerejo, eds., *Complexity Sciences: Theoretical and empirical approaches to social action*. Newcastle upon Tyne: Cambridge Scholars Publishing, pp. 1–6.

Marx, K. (1996). *Capital volume 1 Karl Marx, Frederick Engels Collected Works, Volume 35*. New York: International Publishers.

Maturana, H.R., and Varela, F.J. (1980). *Autopoiesis and Cognition: The realization of the living*. Dordrecht; London: D. Reidel.

Maturana, H.R., and Verden-Zöller, G. (2008). *The Origin of Humanness in the Biology of Love*. Exeter: Imprint-Academic.

Matuszek, K.C. (2007). *Der Krieg als autopoietisches System: Die Kriege der Gegenwart und Niklas Luhmanns Systemtheorie*. Wiesbaden: vs Verlag.

McCombs, M.E., and Shaw, D.L. (1972). The agenda-setting function of mass media. *The Public Opinion Quarterly* 36(2), pp. 176–187.

McLuhan, M. (1964). *Understanding Media: The extensions of man*. New York: McGraw-Hill.

McQuail, D. (1992). *Media Performance: Mass communication and the public interest*. London: Sage.

Meraz, S. (2011). Using Time Series Analysis to Measure Intermedia Agenda-setting Influence in Traditional media and Political Blog Networks. *Journalism and Mass Communication Quarterly* 88(1), pp. 176–194.

Messner, M., and DiStaso, M.W. (2008). The Source Cycle: How traditional media and weblogs use each other as sources. *Journalism Studies* 9(3), pp. 447–463.

Messner, M., and Garrison, B. (2011). *Study Shows Some Blogs Affect Traditional News Media Agendas. Newspaper Research Journal* 32(3), pp. 112–126.

Mingers, J. (2001). Information, Meaning, and Communication: An autopoietic approach. In: F. Geyer and J. van der Zouwen, eds., *Sociocybernetics: Complexity, Autopoiesis, and Observation of Social Systems*. Westport, CT: Greenwood Press, pp. 109–123.

Mitchell, A. (2016). Political legitimacy in Japan: A Luhmannian perspective. *Journal of Sociocybernetics* 14(1), pp. 15–27.

Moffitt, B., and Tormey, S. (2014). Rethinking Populism: Politics, mediatisation and political style. *Political Studies* 62(2), pp. 381–397.

Mudde, C., and Rovira Kaltwasser, C., eds. (2012). *Populism in Europe and the Americas: Threat or corrective for democracy?* New York: Cambridge University Press.

Münkler, H. (2001). Terrorismus als Kommunikationsstrategie: Die Botschaft des 11. September. *Internationale Politik* 12, pp. 11–18.

Münkler, H. (2005). *The New Wars*. Cambridge: Polity Press.

Myers, D.D. (1993). New Technology and the 1992 Clinton Presidential Campaign. *American Behavioral Scientist* 37(2), pp. 181–187.

Newman, N., Fletcher, R., Robertson, C.T., Eddy, K., and Nielsen, R.K. (2022). *Reuters Institute Digital News Report 2022*. Reuters Institute for the Study of Journalism. https://reutersinstitute.politics.ox.ac.uk/digital-news-report/2022.

Nguyen, D. (2017). *Europe, the Crisis, and the Internet: A web sphere analysis*. Cham: Springer International Publishing.

Noelle-Neumann, E. (1984). *The Spiral of Silence: Public opinion, our social skin*. Chicago: University of Chicago Press.

Orwell, G. (2000). *Animal Farm: A fairy story*. London: Penguin Books.

Otake, H. (2003). 『日本型ポピュリズム: 政治への期待と幻滅』[Populism in Japan: Hope and disappointment with politics]. Tokyo: Chuokoron-Shinsha.

Otake, H. (2006). 『小泉純一郎ポピュリズムの研究: その戦略と手法』 [Junichiro Koizumi's populism: Its strategy and style]. Tokyo: Toyo Keizai Shinposha.

Paeteau, M. (2019). The Colombian Peace Process and the Complexity of Violence: A sociocybernetic observation. *Current Sociology Monograph* 67(4), pp. 611–624.

Pariser, E. (2011). *The Filter Bubble: What the Internet is hiding from you.* New York: Penguin Press.

Parsons, T. (2012). *The Social System.* New Orleans: Quid Pro Books.

Pask, G. (1978). A Conversation Theoretic Approach to Social Systems. In: F. Geyer, and J. van der Zouwen, eds., *Sociocybernetics: An actor-oriented social systems approach, Volume 1.* Leiden; Boston: Nijhoff Social Sciences Division, pp. 15–26.

Patrikarakos, D. (2017). *War in 140 Characters: How social media is reshaping conflict in the twenty-first century.* New York: Basic Books.

Pierre, J. (2000). Introduction: Understanding governance. In: J. Pierre, ed., *Debating Governance.* Oxford: Oxford University Press, pp. 1–10.

Pierre, J., and Peters, B.G. (2000). *Governance, Politics and the State.* Basingstoke: Palgrave Macmillan.

Pierre, J., and Peters, B.G. (2005). *Governing Complex Societies: Trajectories and Scenarios.* Basingstoke: Palgrave Macmillan.

Pomerantsev, P. (2019). *This Is not Propaganda: Adventures in the war against reality.* New York: Public Affairs.

Pooley, J. (2008). The New History of Mass Communication Research. In: D.W. Park and J. Pooley, eds., *The History of Media and Communication Research,* New York: Peter Lang, pp. 43–69.

Postigo, H. (2009). America Online Volunteers: Lessons from an early co-production community. *International Journal of Cultural Studies* 12(5), pp. 451–469.

Putnam, R.D. (2000). *Bowling Alone: The Collapse and Revival of American Community.* New York: Simon & Schuster.

Qvortrup, L. (2003). *The Hypercomplex Society.* New York: Peter Lang.

Rachman, G. (2017, February 20). *The Authoritarian Wave Reaches the West: When voters feel the system no longer serves their interests, freedom falters.* The Financial Times. https://www.ft.com/content/6b57d7ae-f74a-11e6-bd4e-68d53499ed71.

Reader, B., and Hatcher, J.A. (2012). *Foundations of Community Journalism.* Los Angeles: SAGE.

Reese, S.D., Rutigliano, L., Hyun, K., and Jeong, J. (2007). Mapping the Blogosphere: Professional and citizen-based media in the global news arena. *Journalism* 8(3), pp. 254–280.

Reese, S.D., and Shoemaker, P.J. (2016). A Media Sociology for the Networked Public Sphere: The hierarchy of influences model. *Mass Communication and Society* 19, pp. 389–410.

Rempel, M. (2001). On the Interpenetration of Social Subsystems: A contemporary reconstruction of Parsons and Luhmann. F. Geyer and J. van der Zouwen, eds., *Sociocybernetics: Complexity, Autopoiesis, and Observation of Social Systems*. Westport, CT: Greenwood Press, pp. 89–106.

Rhodes, R.A.W. (1997). *Understanding Governance: Policy Networks Governance, Reflexivity and Accountability*. Buckingham: Open University Press.

Robertson, R. (2007). Hofmannsthal as Sociologist: "Die Briefe des Zurückgekehrten." In: C. Magerski, R. Savage, and C. Weller, Hrsg., *Moderne Begreifen: Zur Paradoxie eines sozio-ästhetischen Deutungsmusters*. Wiesbaden: Deutscher Universitätsverlag, pp. 231–239.

Rosen, J. (1991). Making Journalism More Public. *Communication* 12(4), pp. 267–284.

Rosen, J. (1999). *What are Journalists for?* New Haven: Yale University Press.

Rosenau, J.N., and Czempiel, E.-O., eds. (1992). *Governance without Government: Order and change in world politics*. Cambridge: Cambridge University Press.

Rühl, M. (1969a). *Die Zeitungsredaktion als Organisiertes Soziales System*. Bielefeld: Bertelsmann Universitätsverlag.

Rühl, M. (1969b). Systemdenken und Kommunikationswissenschaft. *Publizistik* 14, pp. 185–206.

Rühl, M. (1980). *Journalismus und Gesellschaft: Bestandsaufnahme und Theorieentwurf*. Mainz: von Hase & Koehler.

Santos, F.P., Lelkes, Y., and Levin, S.A. (2021). Link Recommendation Algorithms and Dynamics of Polarization in Online Social Networks. *PNAS* 118(50) e2102141118. https://doi.org/10.1073/pnas.2102141118.

Scheufele, B.T., and Scheufele, D.A. (2010). Of Spreading Activation, Applicability, and Schemas: Conceptual distinctions and their operational implications for measuring frames and framing Effects. In: P. D'Angelo and J.A. Kuypers, eds., *Doing News Framing Analysis: Empirical and theoretical perspectives*. New York: Routledge.

Schmitt, C. (2007). *The Concept of the Political*. Chicago and London: University of Chicago Press.

Schneider, W.L. (2007). Religiopolitischer Terrorismus als Parasit. In: T. Kron and M. Reddig, Hrsg., *Analysen des Transnationalen Terrorismus: Soziologische Perspektiven*. Wiesbaden: vs Verlag für Sozialwissenschaften, pp. 125–165.

Scholl, A., and Weischenberg, S. (1998). *Journalismus in der Gesellschaft: Theorie, Methodologie und Empirie*. Opladen: Westdeutscher Verlag.

Schutz, A. (1971). *The Problem of Social Reality*. Hague: M. Nijhoff.

Schutz, A., and Luckmann, T. (1974). *The Structures of the Life-World*. London: Heinemann.

Scott, B. (2001). Gordon Pask's Conversation Theory: A domain independent constructivist mode of human knowing. *Foundations of Science* 6, pp. 343–360.

Scott, B. (2021). *Cybernetics for the Social Sciences*. Leiden; Boston: Brill.

Shannon, C.E., and Weaver, W. (1963). *The Mathematical Theory of Communication.* Urbana: University of Illinois Press.

Shearer, E. (2021, January 12). *More than eight-in-ten Americans get News from Digital Devices.* Pew Research Center. https://www.pewresearch.org/fact-tank/2021/01/12/more-than-eight-in-ten-americans-get-news-from-digital-devices/.

Shoemaker, P.J., and Leese, S.D. (2014). *Mediating the Message in the 21st Century: A media sociology perspective.* New York: Routledge.

Shoemaker, P.J., and Vos, T.P. (2009). *Gatekeeping Theory.* New York; London: Routledge.

Sidorova, K., Peniche Pavía, F., and Rivero Pérez, A.K. (2020). Languaging to Trigger Change: Second-order intercultural conversations with urban youth of Maya descent. *Journal of Sociocybernetics* 17(1), pp. 65–86.

Simmel, G. (1950). *The Sociology of Georg Simmel.* Glencoe, Ill.: Free Press.

Simmel, G. (2007). The Philosophy of Landscape. *Theory, Culture & Society* 24(7–8), pp. 20–29.

Simmel, G. (2009). *Sociology: Inquiries into the construction of social Forms.* Leiden: Brill Academic Publishers.

Simon, F.B. (2002). Was ist Terrorismus? Versuch einer Definition. In: D. Baecker, P. Krieg, and F.B. Simon, Hrsg., *Terror im System: der 11. September 2001 und die Folgen.* Heidelberg: Carl-Auer- Systeme-Verlag, pp. 12–31.

Simon, F.B. (2004). *Patterns of War: Systemic aspects of deadly conflicts.* Heidelberg: Carl-Auer-Systeme- Verlag.

Singer, P.W., and Brooking, E.T. (2018). *Likewar: The weaponization of social media.* Boston: Houghton Mifflin Harcourt.

Slauter, W. (2015). The Rise of the Newspaper. In: R.R. John and J. Silberstein-Loeb, *Making News: The political economy of journalism in Britain and America from the Glorious Revolution to the Internet.* Oxford: Oxford University Press.

Snow, D., and Moffitt, B. (2012). Straddling the Divide: Mainstream populism and conservation in Howard's Australia and Harper's Canada. *Commonwealth and Comparative Politics* 50(3), pp. 271–292.

Solutions Journalism Network. (n.d.). *What Is Solutions Journalism?* https://www.solutionsjournalism.org/about/solutionsjournalism.

Sonenshine, T. (1997). Is Everyone a Journalist? *American Journalism Review* October, pp. 11–12.

Sontag, S. (2007). *At the Same Time: Essays and speeches.* New York: Farrar Straus Giroux.

Spencer-Brown, G. (2021). *Laws of Form.* Leipzig: Bohmeier Verlag.

Sproule, J.M. (1997). *Propaganda and Democracy: The American experience of media and mass persuasion,* Cambridge: Cambridge University Press.

Steinberg, C. (1980). *TV Facts.* New York: Facts on File.

Stepanova, E. (2008). *Terrorism in Asymmetrical Conflict: Ideological and structural aspects,* Oxford: Oxford University Press.

Stuart, C. (2013). *Secrets of Crewe House: The story of a famous campaign*. Miami: HardPress Publishing.

Taekke, J. (2019). Acquisition of New Communication Media and Social (Dis)connectivity. *Current Sociology Monograph* 67(4), pp. 579–593.

Taekke, J. (2022). Algorithmic Differentiation of Society – a Luhmann perspective on the societal impact of digital media. *Journal of Sociocybernetics* 18(1), pp. 1–23.

Taggart, P. (1995). New Populist Parties in Western Europe. *Western European Politics* 18(1), pp. 34–51.

Taggart, P. (2000). *Populism*. Philadelphia: Open University Press.

Taggart, P. (2002). Populism and the pathology of representative politics. In: Y. Mény and Y. Surel, eds., *Democracies and the Populist Challenge*. Basingstoke: Palgrave Macmillan, pp. 62–80.

Takahashi, T. (2015a). Populism and Moralization of Politics in the Age of Systemic Crisis: A sociocybernetic case study of Japanese politics. *The Chuo Law Review* 122(11/12), pp. 1–24.

Takahashi, T. (2015b). Political Crisis and Societal Governance: How media can be societal media? *Journal of Sociocybernetics* 13(2), pp. 84–92.

Takahashi, T. (2019). Governing and Societal Media for Building Resilience: A sociocybernetic study of the disaster recovery in Japan. *Current Sociology Monograph* 67(4), pp. 594–610.

Takahashi, T. (2020). Multilevel Cooperation and Societal Resilience in Disaster Response: A case study of the 2011 disaster in Japan. In: P.E. Almaguer Kalixto, Maria José González Ordovás, and Chaime Marcuello Servós, eds., *Políticas Públicas y Sociales: ¿Ideología, Idolatría o Propaganda?: La globalización social, económica y jurídica*, Zaragoza: Universidad de Zaragoza, pp. 35–46.

Taylor, P.M. (1999). *British Propaganda in the Twentieth Century: Selling democracy*, Edinburgh: Edinburgh University Press.

Tsagarousianou, R. (2000). Electronic Democracy in Practice: One, two, three ... countless variants. *Revue Hermès* 26–27, pp. 233–246.

Tsagarousianou, R., Tambini and, D., and Bryan, C., eds. (1998). *Cyberdemocracy: Technology, cities and civic networks*. London: Routledge.

Turkle, S. (2011). *Alone Together: Why we expect more from technology and less from each other*. New York: Basic Books.

UNDRR (United Nations Office for Disaster Risk Reduction). (2017). *Resilience*. https:// www.undrr.org/terminology/resilience.

Valéry, P. (1989). *The Outlook for Intelligence*, Princeton, N.J.: Princeton University Press.

Van Alstyne, M., and Brynjolfsson, E. (1996). Electronic Communities: Global village or cyberbalkans? (Best Theme Paper). In: *ICIS 1996 Proceedings*. 5. https://aisel.ais net.org/icis1996/5.

Von Foerster, H. (2003). *Understanding Understanding*. New York: Springer.

Wallsten, K. (2007). Agenda Setting and the Blogosphere: An analysis of the relationship between mainstream media and political blogs. *Review of Policy Research* 24(6), pp. 567–587.

Watson, B.R. (2012). Bloggers Rely on Sources Outside Traditional Media. *Newspaper Research Journal* 33(4), pp. 20–33.

Watzlawick, P., Bavelas, J.B., and Jackson, D.D. (2011). *Pragmatics of Human Communication: A study of interactional patterns, pathologies, and paradoxes.* New York: W.W. Norton.

Weber, M. (2004). *The Essential Weber: A reader.* London: Routledge.

Weber, M. (2008). *Max Weber's Complete Writings on Academic and Political Vocations.* New York: Algora Publishing.

Weber, M. (2016). Geschäftsbericht der Deutschen Gesellschaft für Soziologie. *Max Weber Gesamtausgabe, Band 13*. Tübingen: J.C.B. Mohr, pp. 256–286.

Wei, L. (2009). Filter Blogs vs. Personal Journals: Understanding the knowledge production gap on the Internet. *Journal of Computer-Mediated Communication* 14, pp. 532–558.

Weischenberg, S. (1990). Das Paradigm Journalistik. *Publizistik* 35(1), pp. 45–61.

Weischenberg, S. (1994). Journalismus als soziales System. In: K. Merten, S.J. Schmidt and S. Weischenberg, Hrsg., *Die Wirklichkeit der Medien*. Opladen: Westdeutscher Verlag, pp. 427–454.

Weischenberg, S. (2004). *Journalistik: Medienkommunikation: Theorie und Praxis Band 1: Mediensysteme – Medienethik – Medieninstitutionen*. Wiesbaden: vs Verlag für Sozialwissenschaften.

Wittgenstein, L. (2014). *Tractatus Logico-philosophicus*. London: Routledge.

Wenzel, A. (2020). *Community-Centered Journalism: Engaging people, exploring solutions, and building trust.* Urbana: University of Illinois Press.

Zaller, J. (2003). A New Standard of News Quality: Burglar Alarms for the Monitorial Citizen. *Political Communication* 20, pp. 109–130.